Barbara Jo Brothers
Editor

The Personhood
of the Therapist

The Personhood of the Therapist has been co-published simultaneously as *Journal of Couples Therapy*, Volume 9, Numbers 3/4 2000.

Pre-Publication
REVIEWS,
COMMENTARIES,
EVALUATIONS . . .

"**A**ccording to this book the word 'personhood' was invented by Virginia Satir, and her spirit hovers over the whole of this book. Satir is one of the great humanistic heroines, in my opinion, emphasising as she did the need for the therapist to be genuinely present in the encounter with another person, couple or family. It is clear that Barbara Jo Brothers has a very deep appreciation and understanding of Satir's work. All chapters share a respect for the person–both the person of the therapist and the person of the client. This is a book which has much to offer for the therapist who wants to use his or her self to the full in their work."

John Rowan, BA, MAHPP
FBPsS, FBAC
Independent Consultant
United Kingdom

More advance
REVIEWS, COMMENTARIES, EVALUATIONS . . .

"**B**arbara Jo Brothers provides us with a fine collection of writings about how the therapist's self-development forms the foundation for successful psychotherapy. Centering around the ground-breaking work of Virginia Satir, this collection reminds us that the power of psychotherapeutic change emerges when the therapist and the client can meet in a human exchange. The strength of *The Personhood of the Therapist* lies in its reminding us of the peerless work of Satir while integrating her viewpoint with stories of therapists' personal journeys. Several contributions offer integrative frameworks weaving Satir's focus on the therapist's growth with the views of other theorists. The power of human growth is drawn in delicate brush strokes when technique is energized by shared risk-taking by therapist and clients. As they explore the parts of their experiences that have tied their emotions and their lives in knots, the therapists and clients exult in the loosening of bound-up energy."

Allen K. Hess, PhD
Distinguished Research Professor
Department Head
Auburn University at Montgomery
Alabama

"This excellent book provides a much needed balance for the scientistic, bottom-line culture which currently predominates in the world of psychotherapy. It calls attention to culture which currently predominates in the world of psychotherapy. It calls attention to the timeless value of relationship in the therapeutic exchange, approaching the issues of the use of self from a variety of perspectives and in many voices, some personal, some theoretical.

Taking off from a well-chosen base of statements by pioneer family therapist Virginia Satir, the book demonstrates the on-going viability of her insights in a series of essays on their contemporary applications. Among the issues addressed are: The personhood of the therapist as healing agent (including qualities such as self-knowledge, developed awareness, breadth of experience, willingness to self-disclose, courage to take reasonable risks, a sense of spirituality, and the continuity of the therapist's life and work); therapy as education; therapy as art; the importance of right hemisphere exchanges for healing; truth, congruence and transcendence as therapeutic objectives; the recognition that all people are of equal value; and the utterly systemic nature of the therapeutic encounter.

The *Personhood of the Therapist* delivers its core message–the importance of the integration of the therapist's life and work–through offering its readers new ideas for clinical practice as well as insights into their personal relationships."

Phoebe Snover Prosky, MSW
Director of Training
A Center for the Awareness of Pattern
Freeport, Maine

"**T**his book contains valuable reminders of timeless principles in psychotherapy, most notably that love is at the core of effective therapy. The book utilizes a variety of methods, case examples, introspection, theorizing, interviews–to communicate to the reader. Particularly thought-provoking is Lander and Nahan's chapter on integrity.

The carpenter has a hammer, the surgeon has a scalpel, and the therapist has the self. These chapters will surely enhance the instrumentality of the therapist's self, especially the family therapist."

Jeffrey A. Hayes, PhD
Associate Professor
of Counseling Psychology
Pennsylvania State University

"**F**illing a gap in the literature on the development of therapists, Barbara Jo Brothers gathers together the insights of seasoned therapists on their use of their personhood in therapy, as they enter the private world of their clients. The personhood of the therapist is often neglected or underemphasized in the training of therapists and often gets lost amidst the eagerness of students to learn techniques and diagnostic methods. Drawing on the works of Virginia Satir and Satir's intellectual heirs, Barbara Jo Brothers combines the personal stories of therapists both about their clients and themselves. I found the sections on the growth that occurs in facing one's own life crises and how this can positively impact therapy to be most helpful. This book has much to offer both beginning and seasoned therapists."

Jon K. Reid, PhD
Associate Professor/Chair
Department of Psychology
and Counseling
Licensed Professional Counselor
Licensed Marriage
and Family Therapist
Certified Grief Therapist
by the Association for Death Education
and Counseling (ADEC)
Southeastern Oklahoma
State University
Dept. of Psychology and Counseling
Durant, Oklahoma

The Haworth Press, Inc.

The Personhood
of the Therapist

The Personhood of the Therapist has been co-published simultaneously as *Journal of Couples Therapy*, Volume 9, Numbers 3/4 2000.

The Journal of Couples Therapy Monographic "Separates"

Below is a list of "separates," which in serials librarianship means a special issue simultaneously published as a special journal issue or double-issue and as a "separate" hardbound monograph. (This is a format which we also call a "DocuSerial.")

"Separates" are published because specialized libraries or professionals may wish to purchase a specific thematic issue by itself in a format which can be separately cataloged and shelved, as opposed to purchasing the journal on an on-going basis. Faculty members may also more easily consider a "separate" for classroom adoption.

"Separates" are carefully classified separately with the major book jobbers so that the journal tie-in can be noted on new book order slips to avoid duplicate purchasing.

You may wish to visit Haworth's website at . . .

http://www.HaworthPress.com

. . . to search our online catalog for complete tables of contents of these separates and related publications.

You may also call 1-800-HAWORTH (outside US/Canada: 607-722-5857), or Fax 1-800-895-0582 (outside US/Canada: 607-771-0012), or e-mail at:

getinfo@haworthpressinc.com

The Personhood of the Therapist, edited by Barbara Jo Brothers, MSW, BCSW (Vol. 9, No. 3/4, 2000). *Through suggestions, techniques, examples, and case studies, this book will help you develop a great sense of openness about yourself and your feelings, enabling you to offer clients more effective services.*

Couples Connecting: Prerequisites of Intimacy, edited by Barbara Jo Brothers, MSW, BCSW (Vol. 9, No. 1/2, 2000). *"Brothers views marriage as an ideal context for the psychological and spiritual evolution of human beings, and invites therapists to reflect on the role they can play in facilitating this. Readers are sure to recognize their clients among the examples given and to return to their work with a renewed vision of the possibilities for growth and change." (Eleanor D. Macklin, PhD, Emeritus Professor and former Director of the Marriage and Family Therapy program, Syracuse University, New York)*

Couples Therapy in Managed Care: Facing the Crisis, edited by Barbara Jo Brothers, MSW, BCSW (Vol. 8, No. 3/4, 1999). *Provides social workers, psychologists, and counselors with an overview of the negative effects of the managed care industry on the quality of mental health care. Within this book, you will discover the paradoxes that occur with the mixing of business principles and service principles and find valuable suggestions on how you can creatively cope within the managed care context. With* Couples Therapy in Managed Care, *you will learn how you can remain true to your own integrity and still get paid for your work and offer quality services within the current context of managed care.*

Couples and Pregnancy: Welcome, Unwelcome, and In-Between, edited by Barbara Jo Brothers, MSW, BCSW (Vol. 8, No. 2, 1999). *Gain valuable insight into how pregnancy and birth have a profound psychological effect on the parents' relationship, especially on their experience of intimacy.*

Couples, Trauma, and Catastrophes, edited by Barbara Jo Brothers, MSW, BCSW (Vol. 7, No. 4, 1998). *Helps therapists and counselors working with couples facing major crises and trauma.*

Couples: A Medley of Models, edited by Barbara Jo Brothers, MSW, BCSW, BCD (Vol. 7, No. 2/3, 1998). *"A wonderful set of authors who illuminate different corners of relationships. This book belongs on your shelf . . . but only after you've read it and loved it." (Derek Paar, PhD, Associate Professor of Psychology, Springfield College, Massachusetts)*

When One Partner Is Willing and the Other Is Not, edited by Barbara Jo Brothers, MSW (Vol. 7, No. 1, 1997). *"An engaging variety of insightful perspectives on resistance in couples therapy."* *(Stan Taubman, DSW, Director of Managed Care, Alameda County Behavioral Health Care Service, Berkeley, California; Author,* Ending the Struggle Against Yourself)

Couples and the Tao of Congruence, edited by Barbara Jo Brothers, MSW, BCSW (Vol. 6, No. 3/4, 1996). *"A library of information linking Virginia Satir's teaching and practice of creative improvement in human relations and the Tao of Congruence. . . . A stimulating reader."* *(Josephine A. Bates, DSW, BD, retired mental health researcher and family counselor, Lake Preston, South Dakota)*

Couples and Change, edited by Barbara Jo Brothers, MSW, BCSW (Vol. 6, No. 1/2, 1996). *This enlightening book presents readers with Satirs observations–observations that show the difference between thinking with systems in mind and thinking linearly–of process, interrelatedness, and attitudes.*

Couples and Countertransference, edited by Barbara Jo Brothers, MSW, BCSW (Vol. 5, No. 3, 1995). *"I would recommend this book to beginning and advanced couple therapists as well as to social workers and psychologists. . . . This book is a wealth of information."* *(International Transactional Analysis Association)*

Couples: Building Bridges, edited by Barbara Jo Brothers, MSW, BCSW (Vol. 5, No. 4, 1996). *"This work should be included in the library of anyone considering to be a therapist or who is one or who is fascinated by the terminology and conceptualizations which the study of marriage utilizes."* *(Irv Loev, PhD, MSW-ACP, LPC, LMFT, private practitioner)*

Power and Partnering, edited by Barbara Jo Brothers, MSW, BCSW (Vol. 5, No. 1/2, 1995). *"Appeals to therapists and lay people who find themselves drawn to the works of Virginia Satir and Carl Jung. Includes stories and research data satisfying the tastes of both left- and right-brained readers."* *(Virginia O. Felder, ThM, Licensed Marriage and Family Therapist, private practice, Atlanta, Georgia)*

Surpassing Threats and Rewards: Newer Plateaus for Couples and Coupling, edited by Barbara Jo Brothers, MSW, BCSW (Vol. 4, No. 3/4, 1995). *Explores the dynamics of discord, rejection, and blame in the coupling process and provides practical information to help readers understand marital dissatisfaction and how this dissatisfaction manifests itself in relationships.*

Attraction and Attachment: Understanding Styles of Relationships, edited by Barbara Jo Brothers, MSW, BCSW (Vol. 4, No. 1/2, 1994). *"Ideas on working effectively with couples. . . . I strongly recommend this book for those who want to have a better understanding of the complex dynamics of couples and couples therapy."* *(Gilbert J. Greene, PhD, ACSW, Associate Professor, College of Social Work, The Ohio State University)*

Peace, War, and Mental Health: Couples Therapists Look at the Dynamics, edited by Barbara Jo Brothers, MSW, BCSW (Vol. 3, No. 4, 1993). *Discover how issues of world war and peace relate to the dynamics of couples therapy in this thought-provoking book.*

Couples Therapy, Multiple Perspectives: In Search of Universal Threads, edited by Barbara Jo Brothers, MSW, BCSW (Vol. 3, No. 2/3, 1993). *"A very sizeable team of couples therapists has scoured the countryside in search of the most effective methods for helping couples improve their relationships. . . . The bibliographies are a treasury of worthwhile references."* *(John F. Sullivan, EdS, Marriage and Family Counselor in Private Practice, Newburgh, New York)*

Spirituality and Couples: Heart and Soul in the Therapy Process, edited by Barbara Jo Brothers, MSW, BCSW (Vol. 3, No. 1, 1993). *"Provides an array of reflections particularly for therapists beginning to address spirituality in the therapeutic process."* *(Journal of Family Psychotherapy)*

Equal Partnering: A Feminine Perspective, edited by Barbara Jo Brothers, MSW, BCSW (Vol. 2, No. 4, 1992). *Designed to help couples, married or not, understand how to achieve a balanced, equal partnership.*

Coupling . . . What Makes Permanence? edited by Barbara Jo Brothers, MSW, BCSW (Vol. 2, No. 3, 1991). *"Explores what it is that makes for a relationship in which each partner can grow and develop while remaining attached to another." (The British Journal of Psychiatry)*

Virginia Satir: Foundational Ideas, edited by Barbara Jo Brothers, MSW, BCSW (Vol. 2, No. 1/2, 1991). *"The most thorough conglomeration of her ideas available today. Done in the intimate, yet clear fashion you would expect from Satir herself. . . . Well worth getting your hands damp to pick up this unique collection." (Journal of Family Psychotherapy)*

Intimate Autonomy: Autonomous Intimacy, edited by Barbara Jo Brothers, MSW, BCSW (Vol. 1, No. 3/4, 1991). *"A fine collection of chapters on one of the most difficult of human tasks–getting close enough to another to share the warmth and benefits of that closeness without losing what is precious in our separations." (Howard Halpern, PhD, Author, How to Break Your Addiction to a Person)*

Couples on Coupling, edited by Barbara Jo Brothers, MSW, BCSW (Vol. 1, No. 2, 1990). *"A variety of lenses through which to view relationships, each providing a different angle for seeing patterns, strengths, and problems and for gaining insight into a given couple system." (Suzanne Imes, PhD, Clinical Psychologist, Private Practice, Atlanta, Georgia; Adjunct Assistant Professor of Psychology, Georgia State University)*

The Personhood
of the Therapist

Barbara Jo Brothers
Editor

The Personhood of the Therapist has been co-published simultaneously as *Journal of Couples Therapy*, Volume 9, Numbers 3/4 2000.

The Haworth Press, Inc.
New York • London • Oxford

BS

The Personhood of the Therapist has been co-published simultaneously as *Journal of Couples Therapy*, Volume 9, Numbers 3/4 2000.

The development, preparation, and publication of this work has been undertaken with great care. However, the publisher, employees, editors, and agents of The Haworth Press and all imprints of The Haworth Press, Inc., including The Haworth Medical Press® and Pharmaceutical Products Press®, are not responsible for any errors contained herein or for consequences that may ensue from use of materials or information contained in this work. Opinions expressed by the author(s) are not necessarily those of The Haworth Press, Inc.

The Haworth Press, Inc., 10 Alice Street, Binghamton, NY 13904-1580 USA

Cover design by Thomas J. Mayshock Jr.

Library of Congress Cataloging-in-Publication Data

The personhood of the therapist/Barbara Jo Brothers, editor.
     p. cm.
     "Has been co-published simultaneously as Journal of couples therapy, volume 9, numbers 3/4 2000."
     Includes bibliographical references and index.
     ISBN 0-7890-1166-2 (alk. paper)–ISBN 0-7890-1167-0 (alk. paper)
     1. Therapist and patient–Case studies. 2. Interpersonal relations–Case studies. 3. Psychotherapy–Case studies. I. Brothers, Barbara Jo, 1940- II. Journal of couples therapy.
RC480.5 .P4514 2000
616.89'14–dc21

00-059674

4/18/02

Indexing, Abstracting & Website/Internet Coverage

This section provides you with a list of major indexing & abstracting services. That is to say, each service began covering this periodical during the year noted in the right column. Most Websites which are listed below have indicated that they will either post, disseminate, compile, archive, cite or alert their own Website users with research-based content from this work. (This list is as current as the copyright date of this publication.)

Abstracting, Website/Indexing Coverage .... Year When Coverage Began

- *Abstracts of Research in Pastoral Care & Counseling* **1991**

- *BUBL Information Service: An Internet-based Information Service for the UK Higher Education Community <URL:http://bubl.ac.uk/>* **1995**

- *CNPIEC Reference Guide: Chinese Directory of Foreign Periodicals* **1995**

- *Family Studies Database (online and CD/ROM)* **1995**

- *Family Violence & Sexual Assault Bulletin* **1991**

- *FINDEX <www.publist.com>* **1999**

- *Mental Health Abstracts (online through DIALOG)* **1991**

- *Referativnyi Zhurnal (Abstracts Journal of the All-Russian Institute of Scientific and Technical Information)* **1991**

- *Social Services Abstracts <www.csa.com>* **1991**

- *Social Work Abstracts* **1991**

- *Sociological Abstracts (SA) <www.csa.com>* **1991**

- *Studies on Women Abstracts* **1991**

- *Violence and Abuse Abstracts: A Review of Current Literature on Interpersonal Violence (VAA)* **1994**

Special Bibliographic Notes related to special journal issues
(separates) and indexing/abstracting:

- indexing/abstracting services in this list will also cover material in any "separate" that is co-published simultaneously with Haworth's special thematic journal issue or DocuSerial. Indexing/abstracting usually covers material at the article/chapter level.
- monographic co-editions are intended for either non-subscribers or libraries which intend to purchase a second copy for their circulating collections.
- monographic co-editions are reported to all jobbers/wholesalers/approval plans. The source journal is listed as the "series" to assist the prevention of duplicate purchasing in the same manner utilized for books-in-series.
- to facilitate user/access services all indexing/abstracting services are encouraged to utilize the co-indexing entry note indicated at the bottom of the first page of each article/chapter/contribution.
- this is intended to assist a library user of any reference tool (whether print, electronic, online, or CD-ROM) to locate the monographic version if the library has purchased this version but not a subscription to the source journal.
- individual articles/chapters in any Haworth publication are also available through the Haworth Document Delivery Service (HDDS).

The Personhood of the Therapist

CONTENTS

ABOUT THE EDITOR

Barbara Jo Brothers, MSW, BCD, a Diplomate in Clinical Social Work, National Association of Social Workers, is in private practice in New Orleans. She received her BA from the University of Texas and her MSW from Tulane University, where she is currently on the faculty. She was Editor of *The Newsletter of the American Academy of Psychotherapists* from 1976 to 1985, and was Associate Editor of *Voices: The Art and Science of Psychotherapy* from 1979 to 1989. She has 30 years of experience, in both the public and private sectors, helping people to form skills that will enable them to connect emotionally. The author of numerous articles and book chapters on authenticity in human relating, she has advocated healthy, congruent communication that builds intimacy as opposed to destructive, incongruent communication which blocks intimacy. In addition to her many years of direct work with couples and families, Ms. Brothers has led numerous workshops on teaching communication in families and has also played an integral role in the development of training programs in family therapy for mental health workers throughout the Louisiana state mental health system. She is a board member of the Institute for International Connections, a non-profit organization for cross-cultural professional development focused on training and cross-cultural exchange with psychotherapists in Russia, republics once part of what used to be the Soviet Union, and other Eastern European countries.

The Personhood of the Therapist: Effect on Systems

Virginia Satir

Annotations by Barbara Jo Brothers, Editor

EDITOR'S NOTE. In the following excerpts from the beginning of Virginia Satir's first Process Community (Avanta Process Community I, Crested Butte, Colorado, August 1981), and some of her writings, we can see the reason for this theme on personhood. It was Virginia's conviction that therapy actually revolves around personhood–the use of the essential self of the therapist for change in couples, the model for couples to learn to engage, authentic self to authentic self.

AWARENESS NOT TECHNIQUE

[From *Helping Families to Change:*]

To be useful, any technique must emanate from what is going on at that moment in time because it seems to fit, and it is effective only within a context of trust. I cannot overemphasize that point. This is why I cannot teach people techniques, I can only teach them some ways in which they can *use themselves* when certain thing happen. So I could never teach you or anybody "how to do family therapy." As the leader, I teach people by *helping them to come to their own awareness* and to become familiar with the kinds of interaction phenomena that people are involved in.

(1975, p. 136)

NOTE: In other words, Virginia never gave her students fish, she taught them how *to fish. Rather than doling out techniques, she taught*

[Haworth co-indexing entry note]: "The Personhood of the Therapist: Effect on Systems." Satir, Virginia. Co-published simultaneously in *Journal of Couples Therapy* (The Haworth Press, Inc.) Vol. 9, No. 3/4, 2000, pp. 1-14; and: *The Personhood of the Therapist* (ed: Barbara Jo Brothers) The Haworth Press, Inc., 2000, pp. 1-14.

how to fish their own depths for authenticity and how to recognize the constructive style of interaction between a couple–how to discern be-tween that which builds walls versus that which build bridges.

Virginia was always working on her students as persons. *Under-standing that the therapist is a part of the system in any given family therapy context, she worked on helping her student therapist to be-come a fine instrument. As described in her book written with Mi-chele Baldwin (Satir and Baldwin, 1983), her goal was to teach use of the self of the therapist. This meant developing enough self-aware-ness and self worth awareness to be able to communicate therapeuti-cally with self (internally) as well as the other.*

[From *Use of Self in Therapy*]

> Common sense dictates that the therapist and the patient must inevitably impact one another as human beings. This involve-ment of the therapist's "self," or "personhood," occurs regard-less of, and in addition to, the treatment philosophy or the ap-proach Techniques and approaches are tools. They come out differently in different hands . . .
>
> . . . I have learned that when I am fully present with the patient or family, I can move therapeutically with much greater ease. I can simultaneously reach the depths to which I need to go, and at the same time honor the fragility, the power and the sacredness of life in the other. When I am in touch with myself, my feelings, my thoughts, with what I see and hear, I am grow-ing toward becoming a more integrated self. I am more congru-ent, I am more "whole," and I am able to make greater contact with the other person . . . In a nutshell, what I have been describ-ing are therapists who put their *personhood* and that of their patients first . . .
>
> . . . the whole therapeutic process must be aimed at opening up the healing potential within the patient or the client. Nothing really changes until that healing potential is opened. *The way is through the meeting of the deepest self of the therapist with the deepest self of the person, patient or client* [italics mine]. When this occurs, it creates a context of vulnerability–of openness to change . . .

(1987, p. 23-25)

NOTE: In the following excerpt from Virginia's first Process Community, she is demonstrating how and why the personhood of the therapist is an integral part of the therapy process. This excerpt comes from the very beginning of the seminar. In the following interaction with Cathy, a therapist/trainee, Virginia is setting the tone for the seminar, building a nurturing context, demonstrating the procedure the group can expect, and delivering content all at the same time.

INTRODUCTORY EXPLANATION–
BEGINNING THE SEMINAR

I will tell you another reason why I ask people to come to the front of the group to talk about what they want [from the seminar]. I found out some time ago that if I'm outside the presence boundary of people and they're outside of mine, the chances for hallucinating increase and the chances for being able to feel connected decrease . . . So I want to have the best opportunity to see and hear people . . . and besides every once in a while I get lonely, I like it [when I am engaged with an individual trainee].

For those of you who are making your living being change artists called therapists, if you were to have in your consciousness the fact that when you meet people, you meet them always at the edge of their presence boundary . . .

(1981, p. 1)

CONSULTATION WITH CASE EXAMPLE:
"THE SYSTEM EXISTS"

How many of you make your living through therapizing . . . or counseling, they're the same thing . . . or giving advice? Well you always run into the fact that you always are smarter at looking at somebody else [than yourself]. Have you noticed that? Always. And I think we need to remember that. We can always see something there that we can't see in our ourselves, and that is neither good nor bad. It is simply because–when God made us, He forgot something, and next time he makes a human being, I want to have a consultation. There should be a third arm that could be out here with eyes and ears in it and a swivel–you wouldn't have all the problems . . .

. . . (Cathy talks about also being stuck in working with families, and Virginia asks for an example.)

If I can see you work, I might have an idea of how to deal [with this]. I'd like you to tell me of an instance where you saw yourself getting stuck.

Cathy: It happens all the time.

Virginia: No, I can't believe that, because I do not believe it happens all the time. I believe it happens enough times so you think it is all the time. We have to watch that, what people say. Would you believe that for her it happens all the time? Of course not.

Cathy: Well, I was just working with a family the other day, and the daughter had . . .

Virginia: While you are talking, I am going to tell you how my mind works. See, we have only got 20 hours and I have got 20 years of stuff to give you. All right, you are working with a family, and already I know you had, I don't know if they were there–but when you are talking about the family–you are talking about an adult male, and an adult female and at least one child.

Cathy: She was a grown child.

Virginia: Is this all there is in the family?

Cathy: No, there's a sister. Two girls. The child is a female–they are both adult now, they are in their twenties, and the woman in question that I am specifically looking at–she had a psychiatric–

Virginia: What is her age?

Cathy: Twenty-seven.

Virginia: And can you give her a name? It doesn't have to be her own name.

Cathy: Cindy.

Virginia: And this one? [Drawing on blackboard.]

Cathy: Dianne.

Virginia: How old?

Cathy: She is about twenty-three.

Virginia: And this one?

Cathy: Joe.

Virginia: I always put [men] on this side (drawing on board), I don't know why. I stay away from "mother" and "father," because that is only a role.

Cathy: This is June.

Virginia: How old is June?

Cathy: She is almost 60. She is about 58.

Virginia: That is Joe, and how old is Joe?

Cathy: Joe is 60.

Virginia: Ok, now then, you are talking about something. Remember where this came from. This came from Cathy saying that she felt stuck. So this person is the *star*, the one we call the identified patient. They are always the star. Now maybe their light shines in a different way to people, but if you start thinking star or "identified patient," then it will help you to think of the fact that there is life there that they [the star] want to get out and nobody is seeing it. That is one of the functions of a symptom, is that it is an effort to try to grow. So our star then?

Cathy: Our star is just saying, "All I want to be is honest."

Virginia: And that will be very hard there, right? "Please tell me the truth–at least let's stop saying with one hand this, and the other hand something else." Double-level. And I already smell what's in that family and so do you.

Cathy: And dad is saying, "I know you can do it. I know you can go out and live on your own, and have your own apartment."

Virginia: Period. Yes. Try to avoid–I will tell you what I try, is I try to avoid our dirty language of our profession because it makes me so depressed. I try to use language that will help bring pictures. Now it is fine if you want to have sordid discussion with somebody when you talk about paranoid schizophrenia, latent homosexuality, and all that kind of stuff–[but] it doesn't yield much in the way of information . . . There are some people in the field who think I'm simple because I do that. Well, I am simple. All right, and what does June think?

Cathy: "Oh, please don't disappoint me again."

Virginia: Oh, yes, yes. "You are all I have. You are the one who makes my world significant."

Cathy: She is also saying, "You are the most disappointing child."

Virginia: Now how can you be disappointed if they don't mean so much? Think about that for a minute. How can you be so disappointed in somebody if they don't mean a lot to you? So what she is telling you is that girl is the reason for her living. She says, "Don't disappoint me," but what it really means–the other part of that is–"Don't disappoint me because you mean so much to me–You are the reason I live." You want me to say something about when she was born?

Cathy: Sure.

Virginia: Well, first of all, this kid, now 27, was born when her mother was 29–I'm making all this up, but this one never expected, ever, to have a beautiful child, more beautiful than she. And she never had any kind of an awareness that she could do any kind of a decent job as mother. So this one [daughter, Cindy] comes along, and she is beautiful–This one [mother, June] doesn't know how to deal with it.

Now she is married to a guy over here [husband, Joe] who doesn't know how to give her support and doesn't know how to hear the pain in her voice because he is so busy putting down his own pain. She knows about this pain. She knows about his pain, but he can't acknowledge it. Tell me, is any of that true?

Cathy: Yeah.

Virginia: It has to be that way from what you told me. Now, he says "keep it up kid," That means, "Make the world and our family look like a happy place." Mother is saying, "Please, you are all I have got. Don't disappoint me or I will die." And she is saying, "For God's sake, get your act together! . . .

Virginia: Now this one over here, this is the main triad in this family. This is the first one, and when this one [daughter, Cindy] came these two [Joe and June] got separated. Now this one [daughter, Dianne] is second, and she is freer than this one [Cindy]–but she has had a whole secret life that the rest of the world does not know anything about. She has to.

Now what I am demonstrating to you is my *knowledge of systems*. Not my knowledge, but how systems work. So tell me how much of that is relevant?

Cathy: Oh, that is very close.

Virginia: Ok. See, once you start to read what is going on there is not that much of a secret. It isn't. It is all very clear, all here in the messages.

Virginia: . . . True or not true?

Cathy: Right on.

Virginia: Sure, because that fits what is going on. Now, I did this for a reason at this point in time. Not to show you how smart I am but to show you that the *system exists.* The system exists and if you understand it, you can read anything, in yourself or in anybody else if you get the chance to do it. It has nothing to do with magic, it has to do with the same thing in the position mode . . . we are at the beginning of knowing how that works.

NOTE: "Position Modes" refers to what Virginia described in other places (1991) as the stress ballet; this is a shifting among four different external ways family members respond to each other: placating, blaming, being super-reasonable or being irrelevant. These incongruent, static external responses are born of internal doubt–questions about self-worth and the stress that accompanies such self-questioning. Too often a given person does not feel good enough about herself or himself to give straight answers or congruent information about internal experience. Instead, the person will give a response that is incongruent with her or his internal experience.

THERAPIST ENTERS FAMILY SYSTEM

Now, then, you come in. Here are the messages, and you come in. Here is the therapist over here, and the messages I heard from you, "I'll help you or else." It is not really a threat in the general sense, but in this family it is a terrible threat, because it says you are going to change that system and it also says that this is translated into control over here. So they are going with two things.

NOTE: Virginia means the following. The family, in response to the therapist's anxiety, is now dealing with two things, in spite of their wish for relief: the upset of change and their fear of the perceived threat of being controlled.

So, they are not going to be controlled by you. Do you think Joe is going to give up his cheerleading? No, not at this time, because he doesn't want to do it. So, control. Now it is supposed to be a loving control. Do you know how to do the loving control business? "It's good for you." Many of us were brought up that way. "And I will do whatever I need to do because it's good for you." Now there are a lot of things that might be good for you; and I know ways to help you be in touch with that . . .

Now, this therapist here is what I would call a committed therapist, because I know you are. Committed therapist, smart, scared sometimes and not always clear on what is going on. And that is nether good nor bad. But it is just the state or condition, right?

So you like this girl. You wish she had different parents. Am I right?

Cathy: Yeah.

Virginia: Of course. Now then, this is a very interesting thing, and I am just kind of getting a little scene here . . . In a sense, it is easy, without meaning to, to suddenly feel these are kind of enemies. Kind of. You know how to say–teachers do it all the time in school, comparing one kid to another by saying, "well, you know, you really do very nice work. Better than Jane, although Jane could do it if she tried." Any of you hear that when you were growing up? Do you hear the putdown in that?

Anyway, all I am talking about now is another level of messages that have nothing to do with your intentions. They have to do with how you really ought to help that girl get somewhere in life. I know that. And I think you will, and maybe before this is over, we will do a role-play of this family, You see, when I started out with her, the star, she tried to bring life to this family because I think this woman [mother, June] never even tried to get what she hoped for. And this man has settled for second-best. I don't know about his physical condition, but I suspect something.

Cathy: Yeah, it seemed he had some.

Virginia: He has either got to have back problem, or he has sexual dysfunctions, because he has got to put so much into being cheery while the inside of him dies. And then he has his anger, I can't imagine him being angry with anybody.

Cathy: No, he is always . . .

Virginia: Of course. He would have to be. Because if he got angry that means that everything would blow up. So you have all sorts of anger coming in for all the things you have to take on in life and the world, the burden on your shoulders while you try to stand up. . . . So it all makes sense. How do you feel right now? Do you already, from this, have some idea about this family?

Cathy: Yes, much clearer ideas.

Virginia: How many of you are interested in the kind of thing that Cathy brought?

I would like to ask you a question; it is a belief question, and there is nothing in whatever you say about it, bad or good. If you do not already know it, do you believe that everything bands together in a system? I think once you have got that belief, what that means is that everything affects everything else. And every family has a focus–everything moves. It turns out, in my opinion anyway, that everything is connected and impacts with everything else. *We can not talk about that family without Cathy [the therapist].* And then, of course, we learn later that we can not talk about that family without Cathy and her [own] father and mother and sister and brother and Joe and his mother and father and brother and sister, and June and so on.

(1981, p. 2-11)

NOTE: *Here, Virginia has just made her point about the importance of the personhood of the therapist. The therapist is* part *of the system. The therapist is not a spectator; therapist and family are all one interacting system. The personhood of the therapist bumps up against the patient. Despite anybody's intent, this is an inherent part of the process. Virginia's experience and observation was that better therapy takes place when the therapist is aware of the fact of (1) the existence of the system and (2) interplay within the system.*

PROCESS IN ALL SYSTEMS

NOTE: *Virginia wanted to make clear the true meaning of "person of the therapist." To do this, she spends time pointing out that each individual person is a system unto themselves–and, therefore, in continual process.*

I would like to make a few comments about the procedure [for the seminar]. What I have found is that *every experience has a dance to it.* That is what I call *process* [writing on the board]. You see . . . your left brain just loves to use process and the right brain says, "Aha, that means a dance." The movements of things that move back and forth. And we are always making a dance because we are always moving, because there is no such thing as being able to stand still. Even if we stand still, our blood runs inside, our heart beats, there is no way we can ever be still. The movement is going on. Some movement is more obvious than other movement. When I go like so [gesture] that is more obvious than if I am just thinking that and not doing. Movement is always going on all over the planet, 24 hours a day and has since the beginning of time.

(1981, p. 25)

WHAT IS PERSONHOOD?

NOTE: One finds mostly oblique definitions of personhood–a word Virginia Satir invented–in Virginia's writings and even in the tran-scribed lectures. She was not interested in creating academic defini-tions; she was occupied with drawing forth the actuality of person-hood–the real experience–in her seminar participants. To describe, on paper, what she means by "person" may be close to impossible. On the other hand, watching her work, one can begin to see how she uses her self to affect whatever other "self" is part of the working context. Anybody with a serious interest in understanding Virginia's work should view several different videotaped sessions in which she is work-ing with families and seminar trainees.

Virginia held human beings in deep reverence. She honored, to her last breath, the human capacity to change, to grow, to surmount ob-stacles, to live. She mourned the failure of so many to choose change, to remain "boxed in" by inertia and fear–a "dark cylinder" filled with hidden, unused potencies instead of daring to become the "star"; a "shining light" (1988, p. 341), free, engaged in the "dance of life" and released from the exhausting pace of the "stress ballet."

She understood the profound implications of our uniqueness, our inherent connectedness, our power to implement life-giving or life-de-stroying processes. This view of the facts of human reality filled her mind, shaped her work, moved her to dare dreams of unity and peace for the human race–and are prerequisite for those who would like to become therapists in the foot steps of Virginia Satir.

ALL PEOPLE ARE EQUAL–EACH PERSON IS UNIQUE

. . . the world is changing here . . . giving out some new possibilities. So now we have the beginnings of another view of how we can look at people . . . we saw Abe Maslow talking and Rollo May talking about that the definition of a relationship is one of equality. Now that sounds peculiar to people, because how can everybody be equal? You know, some are tall, some are short, . . . What that really means is that our navels are equal in the sense that we all came the same way. So, this had to do with value and worth, that people are of value. And they equaled each other in value and manifestation of life force. If we really believe what we are told on the theological level, that we are made in the image or likeness of the Creator, then how can we be unequal? We can put it in any terms we want. So we began to say person equals person because they have navels and because they are manifestations of life force.

This was so new, this important discovery, and at first it brought dismay, How could I, a four-year-old, feel equal to my mother, a 44 year old? How could I, a 45 year old, feel equal to my mother who is seventy years old? How could I, a student feel equal to my professor? [Not] because you have all the same amounts of knowledge or the same age but because you are a manifestation of life force was what it was about.

Now this was discovery, and there were lots of discoveries in relation to that. How, as far as the definition of a person was concerned, what we knew was that a person was unique . . . Every person is a combination of sameness and of differentness to every other person. So it is not that if you love me we will be the same and if you did not love me, you will be different, but the genuine, basic nature of the human being is a combination of sameness and differentness.

That meant then, that there were no duplicates of people. And it also meant something else, think about the fingerprint which I told you about before . . .

YOU AFFECT AND YOU HAVE AN EFFECT

[Once uniqueness is understood and appreciated, the question comes:] . . . So how does harmony come? How you can put the unity between what is the opposite and what is the same. The harmony between the two. How do we put dark and light together, how do we put men and women together, how do we put short and tall together, how do we put different belief systems together, how do we live in a place where people believe differently, and still can have harmony?

. . . Now that, of course, is the picture of a system. And a system, a very older, simplified definition of a system, is action, reaction and interaction, amongst a set of essential variables that develop an order and a sequence for a joint outcome. That is all it is. A simple definition. It means that everything affects everything else, and everything that is bound together for some kind of a survival [action] or outcome has to affect each other. Like a man and woman who have a kid, the kid had to be affected by how the man and woman relate as parents. How they relate to each other and to the little kid, He had to be affected by what he is told, to how he is to relate to them and so on. It has to be. You have an effect, You *affect* and you have an *effect*, and that is about as simple as I can make it.

Now we are just beginning in human circles to accept the concept of system in relation to ourselves. This happens and then that happens and then that happens. A man, woman, and child are in my treatment office and the boy has got a scowl on his face. You have seen that. Sixteen. And mother looks over at his father, and his father is up very straight looking back at the mother like that. And then I see a tear go down her face. That is a systems response. The boy does something, the father looks to the mother to do something and she feels helpless and so she cries. The next part of that is the boy stamps his foot some more and he yells out something that sounds psychotic. Then the father gets helpless, and la, la, la. *What we have been used to doing is freezing something and calling it our analysis [or diagnosis] instead of seeing that this moves.*

(1981, pages 68-72)

NOTE: Virginia is making a critically important point above. She is commenting on the fact that mental health professionals, in making a diagnosis, are, in essence, "freeze-framing" an interaction. Even a description of a system must take into account the system is always in process–is an ever shifting field of response and counter response. This is one reason Virginia did not find diagnosis, in the ordinary sense, particularly useful. She was much more interested in understanding the interactional patterns of a given family system, at the same time, recognizing that what she saw in one moment would be different in the next moment.

PERSONHOOD AND CATEGORIZING

Question [from the audience] about Virginia's view on psychotic people . . .

Let me just say, first of all, that if you would allow me I would like you to restate something. And I will give you the words and see if you feel all right about it. I heard you talk about psychotic people. Would you change that to people who have, at moments in time, psychotic manifestations? Would you say that and see what happens to your throat?–[repeats question using this statement]–How did that feel when you said that? Foreign. Ok, because it is new, because we have been so used to glibly applying labels. Go in hospitals, "go down to that paranoid," "go down to that back injury." "Go down to so and so.

Remember all those words that come out of your mouth reinforce something. Now say it again and see if you have hope–[repeats the question] . . . How did that feel to you when you said that? Different. Of course it does, because *what it does is leave the personhood intact and puts your mind on the condition.* And when you do that, you are not going to give any feedback to people [that they are merely a] category, And so you are freeing the life of that self-worth, in your own mind, to exist, to become your colleague and support to help with the behavior that comes out. The principles are exactly the same.

(1981, p. 189)

ONLY ONE THOUGHT AWAY

[From Virginia's own notes:]

> Positive self worth is only one thought and one action away.
> I am of positive worth because I am a person.
> I am of positive worth because I am a manifestation of life.
> That, we all are.
> When we believe that, the struggle then becomes only the creation of a form to express it.
> Any change creates both a problem and suggests a solution.
> Any change can be a crisis.
> Any crisis offers up possibilities:
> Try to stay where you are,
> Retreat to a "safer" place or *venture into new territory*

(circa 1986)

REFERENCES

Satir, V., Stachowiak, J. & Taschman, H. (1975). *Helping families to change.* New York: Jason Aronson, Inc.

Satir, V. (1981). First process community, Park City, Utah. Unpublished transcript.

Satir, V., & Baldwin, M. (1983). *Satir step by step.* Palo Alto, CA: Science and Behavior Books.

Satir, V. (circa 1986). *Your third birth.* Unpublished manuscript. Santa Barbara, CA: Virginia Satir Archives, Special Collection. Davison Library. University of California.

Satir. V. (1988). *The New peoplemaking.* Mountain View, California: Science and Behavior Books.

Satir, V., Banmen, J., Gerber, J. & Gomori, M. (1991) *The Satir model: Family Therapy and Beyond.* Palo Alto, CA: Science and Behavior Books.

The Nature of Personhood:
Interview with Jean McLendon

Barbara Jo Brothers

EDITOR'S NOTE. "Personhood" is a term invented by Virginia Satir as a way of referring to the unique essence of each particular human being. Honoring personhood was the core of Virginia's work. Jean McLendon was studying with Virginia when I first met her in 1970. Later, she became one of Virginia's most trusted colleagues; Virginia asked Jean to take her place in leading the eighth Process Community in 1988, when Virginia was unable to continue because of illness. The following interview took place August 2, 1999.

SUMMARY. Interview of Jean McLendon by Barbara Jo Brothers on the nature of personhood. Included are concepts from the work of Virginia Satir, thoughts about the importance of heart energy, ways of connecting "at the essence" point, and tapping into the personhood of both therapist and client. *[Article copies available for a fee from The Haworth Document Delivery Service: 1-800-342-9678. E-mail address: <getinfo@haworthpressinc.com> Website: <http://www.HaworthPress.com>]*

KEYWORDS. Personhood, person, essence, heart energy, interpersonal process patterns, pleasure, pain

Jean McLendon, MSW, CCSW, is Director of Training for the "Satir System Performance Development Program," a year-long professional development program for psychotherapists and organizational change specialists. She serves on the faculties of the Avanta Network, Inc., The Satir Institute of the Southeast, Inc. and The International Institute for the Study of Systems Renewal, Inc., affiliated with Antioch University's Seattle based "Whole Systems Design" graduate program.

Address correspondence to: Jean McLendon, 2013 South Lakeshore Drive, Chapel Hill, NC 27514 (E-mail: jean@satir.org).

[Haworth co-indexing entry note]: "The Nature of Personhood: Interview with Jean McLendon." Brothers, Barbara Jo. Co-published simultaneously in *Journal of Couples Therapy* (The Haworth Press, Inc.) Vol. 9, No. 3/4, 2000, pp. 15-28; and: *The Personhood of the Therapist* (ed: Barbara Jo Brothers) The Haworth Press, Inc., 2000, pp. 15-28. Single or multiple copies of this article are available for a fee from The Haworth Document Delivery Service [1-800-342-9678, 9:00 a.m. - 5:00 p.m. (EST). E-mail address: getinfo@haworthpressinc.com].

PERSONHOOD, HEALING, AND HEART ENERGY

BJB: Virginia Satir believed the concept of personhood is essential to healing in family therapy. Give us some of your ideas on the "how-to's" of good therapy.

JM: The way to enter the healing channels is, if you will from my perspective, by way of heart energy.

BJB: Yes.

JM: How do you do it? So I was thinking about that. How do you connect with some one at essences [the essence of both persons–therapist and client]? How do you fit in that kind of space? That is both something that you do internally and gets manifested in how you interact externally with the client. And I was struck by something that my mother [said]–I was just visiting her in the assisted living situation where they all moved in–well, all ten of them. It is a new place and they don't have that many people there yet. But it is like, they have no shared history. And these are elderly people.

I started thinking about the use of the family map as a way–in a way it is a means to build a sense of knowing. And to compensate, if you will, for that lack of history you have with a client that walks in the door. Because when I know the story about Aunt Susie or Grandpa then I know something about that person that you don't really usually know unless you have got a long shared history or an intimate shared history.

But to just hear the story seems like that is not enough either. And one of the things I think Virginia Satir did so well was that she knew how to sift out from narration and show the universals that had to do with life's challenges and life's longings.

BJB: That is a nice way of putting it.

JM: So that is where I think, particularly in this time of managed care because people–you know–everything is fast-paced. Too fast paced.

BJB: Well, everything is also sort of de-humanizing.

JM: That pace does seem to erode the humanness. I think we can, as therapists–if we are skilled, and if we are operating from that core that Virginia Satir was talking about–I think we can do a lot in a short period of time.

BJB: Yes.

JM: Because what we are talking about doing, that is, connecting to a person's real essence as a way to open the channel of that person's healing–for people to have that experience so validating and so supportive: I think there is no limit to the power of that experience.

For me, what is sad is having [that experience without enough time to consolidate it]. The fact is people do get that experience with good therapists but they aren't often able to stay in therapy long enough to really understand how much they participate in the process and what skills they are using that are opening themselves. So it is harder for the process to have a kind of sustainability. Because in a sense the transformation and the support can feel so positive and rich. However, their job–all of our jobs–is to find in our lives, in our families, in our friendships and in our churches or in our whatever, places which open heart energy (especially maybe with ourselves, the therapists). And [to find] the skills; the ways to tap into that positive, nurturing, open, healing kind of energy that is based on, it seems to me, very simply, love. [It is the] experience of love energy moving in and between to [make things] safe. [To make it so that] that I can return to that experience. If I can return to that experience of being genuine–if you have not had much of that [experience] and then you get it with a therapist, it is very moving and very powerful. Then there is how do I learn how to do it without a therapist? That one has got me a little more befuddled.

BJB: In ten sessions.

JM: Right. And maybe it is just people who have got offtrack and need a little help to get back on track [who can move on quickly after the ten sessions] but for people who basically do not know very much, experientially, about getting support, receiving support, opening themselves to be seen, to really be heard, really be [validated]–[those people] have very little experience with this. If that is what really opens the healing channels, they then need help in practicing it.

CONNECTING VERSUS DISCONNECTING

BJB: Do you think Virginia Satir could really help people do that [opening of the healing channels] quicker than the rest of us? Or do you think anybody has to have [a given] amount of practice to be able to keep the channels appropriately open?

JM: I definitely think the amount of practice needed in the change process depends on the person. At least during the time when *I* knew Virginia, a lot of her work was, you know, sort of one time experiences. And it would be a very powerful transformative experience, but what the person was able to carry from that [experience] in terms of manifesting different behaviors, I don't know. And I mean I certainly know people who had very moving family reconstruction experiences and who, you know, continued to struggle years later with difficulties. I mean if you didn't know you would not *know* they'd had a reconstruction. It is not like the reconstruction cured them. And I am sure those people would take nothing for those experiences. So maybe it is a long time sometimes for what is cooking on the inside to really be a real delicacy on the outside. And, again, depending on the strengths of the person and I think really how much they know about getting and receiving support.

BJB: Hmmm

JM: Because everything, I have decided, is easier with support and it is amazing the number of people whose strategy for survival is–because of distrust–to isolate themselves–to withdraw. Or to blame. And so those behaviors do not make it very easy for them to get support.

Anyway, back to the idea of how do we enter that [space] and help open that channel. Not that we could not do it with some clients without a word being spoken. I am sure there are some people who could come in and we could just sit with them. Maybe hold their hand. Look in their eyes and just sit reverently. But, for the most part, people do need to talk about their lives as a way to connect.

And Virginia knew how to take a little bit of story and know how that story could sit in a larger context of people's interpersonal process patterns (what I call them). So no matter the story–if you are doing a family map or if you are listening to what it is a family wants to have happen–she picked up very fast on the universal challenges and longings. She also picked up how the system seemed to manage interpersonally–themselves–in the process of that event. So you would get back to the problem is not the problem; it is the coping. She was listening with about three ears. One, enough of the context to get the universal issue and then also hearing enough to get how the system was operating interpersonally. And that last one–how the system operates in terms of its interpersonal process–seems essential just in terms of what we are just talking about.

If we are going to be in a healing place, in a sense, we can not do it all by ourselves. I mean we are social beings, me/you. So the connection we were talking about with the client and the therapist–those connections–or lack of connections–in the family system are central to how well, in effect, the client can take the family and move it into "real time" [as opposed to "practice time," in the presence of the therapist] with significant family members and friends. So if the system is highly adept at disconnecting and very incompetent at connecting, your client has got their work cut out for them because they cannot do it alone.

BJB: Would you say the incompetence is, generally speaking, lack of familiarity and practice? Or not?

JM: Well, I think there is a lack of familiarity with it. It is not the norm to connect around things–it is the norm to stay distant and protected in that way. Of course, it doesn't protect you from life to stay disconnected but a lot of people surely have become experts at living from a distance.

BJB: Umhm

VIRGINIA SATIR WORKED WITH THE PERSON OF THE THERAPIST

JM: And it is very difficult to access that healing energy when our hearts are living at a distance to these people who are most important to us.

BJB: That's well put. That is true. I am trying to think how this applies to the therapist, too.

JM: In terms of our healing or in terms of our helping access the healing with the client?

BJB: I was thinking more in terms of our own dynamics–coming from the same general population and being vulnerable to the same disconnected norm.

JM: Yes, yes, well, I think that is why Virginia's training programs were so effective. Because she worked with the person of the therapist.

BJB: Yes.

JM: She taught us how to connect. She taught us about how important it was and then she taught us how to do it. And, of course, it wasn't short term training. If you think about it, like, for some of us, it was long term training. But for people who maybe went only to one month long [workshop], or even if they went to a three day workshop, there was the opportunity to, [one], see her connecting and, [two], be an observer to that [connecting] process and learn from it. Also the skills–[to observe and learn] the communication skills.

BJB: From what it looked like to me, it seemed me like a person almost had to spend a whole month [in training with Virginia] to know what she was really talking about. Now that is coming from my first exposure having taken place in my extreme youth. If I had seen her when I had some sense, later on, it might have all leapt into place quicker.

JM: Well, what happened for me the first time I was in a workshop with her, I did manage to be the mother and wife in the simulated family so it was "up close and personal." But what I was struck with was everything she said I knew was true, but no one had ever said it. It had not been said. So I think if I had had no more experience with [the Satir Model], I would have been given some truths that I could not deny and that were very validating of my life. And of my feelings–the value, if you will, of my emotions. And I don't know what more I could have done with just that one experience, but I did know it was true. I think people see it. I said, "Oh, yeah, yeah. Yeah. Right on." Then people go into their offices and then say, but, ok, so now what do I do?" So maybe what is missing is, again, the opportunity to practice and to experience. I have no idea how people learn therapy without having the kind of indepth experience that we had.

The value to me–besides–well, one of the primary values was that I was in one reconstruction after another, after another, after another and another. Therefore, I went to the insides–to the inner system–of so many families–to that intimate core. And from all different angles, as mother, as grandmother, as daughter, as aunt, as sister–and I think that is what helped me learn about–a term which I call "the universality of emotionality." [Role-playing in many family reconstructions] really is a way to learn about what it really means to be a human being. It does not matter the story; it does not matter the culture at the deepest level if you can go through the veils and the fears and the defenses that get constructed in culturally specific kinds of ways. If you just get to the heart of the person or of the family you get it validated time and time again about what Virginia used to say: we all just want to be loved.

WHAT IS "HEART ENERGY"–WHAT IS LOVE?

BJB: Yeah, and that is so simple. People think it can't be true because it is too simple.

JM: Right. I will tell you an interesting story about how simple that is and how hard it is to get. I don't know if when you were with Virginia if she was using the Self Esteem Maintenance Tool Kit?

BJB: Not yet. If she was, she was not calling it that–she might have been using it.

JM: Well, in [the kit] is the courage stick, the wisdom box, the detective hat, the yes/no medallion, the golden key, and the wishing wand. Each of those represented what she believed to be the God-given, if you will, resources that every human has and they are like tools for maintaining our self esteem. Well, I added the heart. Now for years, I knew it was missing and I didn't know about this until Virginia died because, to be honest with you, before she died, as far as I was concerned, the self esteem kit was another–I don't even know what the word is–but kind of a soft, not necessarily well-thought-out, a little too fluffy, too cute or something.

So anyway, it was only after she died that I got into the Self Esteem Tool Kit and created it, got the icons like the literal golden key, a literal courage stick–like visual aids–and then I realized that the heart was missing. And I figured it was an oversight because she certainly knew about it and tried to teach us about it. The interesting thing was this trainee of mine was going to do some stationery [out of which to form a logo]–and, when you are teaching, you can throw a lot of words and people will kind of get the sense of it. She wanted *one* word. And I had said well, the heart is our capacity to be compassionate. And she said aren't you talking about feelings? I said well, yes.

Anyway I never did land on what exactly and succinctly the heart was representing for the self esteem maintenance kit until this summer. And it is, *of course,* the ability to love, period. I can't tell you how long I kind of thought, "Well, exactly what is it?" I mean I know she doesn't have it in the kit. It is not the wisdom; it is something different from the wisdom she used to talk about. How can you really be congruent if you can not love yourself? If you can't from–in the heart–be in a loving and receptive place to the person you are in dialogue with? The easiest thing to have congruence stop, that is, [to stop] the flow, is [to stop] the love energy–the heart to close and distance to be created and blaming to start. I don't know where all this is except to say that yes, I think it is very simple, but it is hard. I'm not dumb. I'm not the brightest person in the world by a long shot, but is like after using this for years, I said, "Oh." Simple.

BJB: When I said "simple," I did not mean easy.

JM: Right. Yes.

BJB: I think Virginia was full of simple stuff that was so simple that people could not understand it.

JM: Well, I think at the level that many of us have stayed with her system I think that is true. She made it look simple. She made it sound simple. She made it look easy. But–and it is a hard one for me now, too, to forget because it is so natural: it is hard to know how much people don't know, when what we know seems so basic.

BJB: Yes. I get caught up short every so often with that.

JM: I do, too. I forget. I get caught up short similarly living in Chapel Hill even though it is in the South. I go to places and I hear–whether it is racial prejudice or whether it is homophobia, or, just on and on. I forget how frightened people are out there in the world.

BJB: Yes.

JM: And that is another thing that closes the heart down.

BJB: Quick.

JM: You bet. You bet. So interestingly enough about the heart, you remember the article I wrote for your journal about the seven "A's" (McLendon, 1996).

BJB: Yes.

JM: I think, at that time, it was six. They kept growing. I have come to the last one and there are seven. The last one is altruism. I don't know if you remember the first one was basically about within the person: awareness, acceptance, and authorship. That is kind of all inside the person. Then you move to the between, which is articulation, and then application in your intimate, close-in relationships. And from there you go to activism, which is carrying the learning from your awareness into culture beyond your own. And there from activism is altruism. Now I have been saying altruism as the seventh for two years and everytime I say it, I say, similarly, it is kind of hard. I believe this is true and that it is different from activism and that it is important for us to know about. To be honest with you, I don't know what I need to know about it to be able to teach about it.

BJB: Every so often, I try to figure out how to define "love" and I have not come up with it yet and maybe altruism is in the same little circle.

JM: Yes. This summer, [I finally came up with something] after spending a week in a monastery and just having time and in a community that was intent on prayer and opening the heart–for me to be still enough and just quiet enough to see what would lift up out of me. That is when I came up with that: altruism is acting from the heart. The motivation is in the heart. I can tell you there is plenty I do that looks like, "Isn't she generous, isn't she blah, blah, blah" that is more about activism and/or applying but not exactly coming from my heart. Not that I don't have my heart participating, but I think altruism is so clearly heart motivated.

BJB: Yes. That is good. I think about that a lot.

JM: Well, maybe that is another [journal] issue: What is love?

BJB: I think it is a pretty good issue, myself and I think it is connected [to the issue at hand] because you started out by talking about loving energy being the–how did you put it?–What is the connecting force? Or the connecting energy?

JM: The loving energy, I think, is the energy that opens the channel to the healing energy and, again, it is like how do we, as therapists, create inside of ourselves, that living healing energy? That is energy of being centered and being balanced and being present and being mindful, and being prayerful, all those. How do we learn to create that in ourselves so we can extend *that* and use *that* as the milieu for our therapy intervention? Whether it is again going back to the family map and getting narratives and connecting those to the universal issues of being humans, to how those issues are represented in the events that are being talked about and then how the interpersonal patterns are holding those events. It is like all of that must happen while the therapist is in a balanced, giving [mode] that is opening, that is heart energy, I think.

And receiving the client. Receiving what? Receiving the self, I guess, of the client.

BJB: You are helping me with a real difficult one I have to see later today.

JM: I have to do one right after us that is real difficult. This will be the third time I have seen her and I feel like she presents with such an incredible mask.

BJB: Mmm

JM: I, I don't know. It is going to be interesting to see when or if I really feel like she relaxes. Which is a part of being in the healing energy, is to let the body–going back to Virginia–the connection with the body is letting the body relax.

BJB: Yes, that is part of the openness.

JM: I don't know whether it has value for whatever might be able to be put into words for this issue you are dealing with, but, in terms of trying again to elicit from the client's story, a handle of her or their or his challenge for being human. [Pause . . .] I could talk about the "P's."

THE SIX "P'S"[1] (MCLENDON, 1998)

I think I talked about that at the Avanta meeting–the "P's." I think you were there, I don't know. I have got them down. It is like there are areas which I am interested in pursuing or keeping my antenna awake for. It is, again, looking for whatever the interpersonal process patterns are, for how the system deals with, number one, pain.

I think about my mother yesterday crying–a woman who does not cry. Who had two blind children in the family she grew up in. All the pressures in the family–two kids that are blind and having to make do in the time of Depression, being a farming family, you just sucked up anything that. . . .

BJB: Oh, yes.

JM: So how did she learn how to deal with pain? As I talk with her, it is like she sucked it up and, course, I think her body paid. So, for her, just being able to cry was like a huge thing for her. So how people deal with pain. Like in that family, you really were not supposed to have it. Relatives dying. Physical pain. Interpersonal pain. Feelings hurt. Ta da ta da ta da. I mean, you could just go on and on. This life has not been created so that any of us could be without pain.

BJB: Certainly hasn't.

JM: And so, again, are patterns–the interpersonal patterns–that have to do with pain–do they help people connect–which would be creating that healing milieu? Or do they support people *dis*connecting? And, too often, pain is a precipitant for disconnecting.

BJB: That's the truth. Those who grew up in households where they were not going to get a comfortable response.

JM: Yep. You learn. You learn to suck it up and it comes out somewhere. It is going to get expressed somewhere in the body, somatically, or in the ways that you communicate. Both.

BJB: Right.

JM: So those "P's." The first one, I think, is very important. What do you find out and how can you help people connect with their pain rather than disconnect? And then, next, which I think is almost equally a challenge for people and that is how they deal with pleasure.

BJB: Oh, yes.

JM: I can't tell you how many couples I work with–young couples–where I think the primary focus is about giving them permission and help in learning how to create pleasure in their life.

BJB: Yes.

JM: I mean, again, it is not real easy. Pleasure can be just as disconnecting as pain and that is the jealousies that come up in families: somebody had a wonderful time, the other one didn't. Or the issues around how much it cost. And, if you came from a kind of work-oriented family like I did–*pleasure* is not thought too well of. If you got pleasure from your work, that was good. But there is something about learning how to be pleasured. Learning how and whether it is [o.k.]–I remember one of my supervisors in my social work training said, "You know, you just don't really appreciate the pleasure of eating." She was really a wonderful supervisor and my ex-husband–I wasn't married to him at this time–anyway, he was, at the time, in Hawaii. I met him and she and he and I would spend a lot of time together and often times it was around food. And it is true. I did not know the pleasure of eating. It was something you did. Kind of like brushing your teeth, you know?

BJB: Well, that kind of goes with that work-oriented thing.

JM: Right.

BJB: You just get this over with quick so you can get back to what you were doing.

JM: Right. Right. So I have since learned the pleasure of eating. It is like the sensual experience of being alive. What a loss when we are not supported to be resonate with that. What a loss.

So there were other "P's" from how the system deals with problems–how it deals with plans, can you count on your family to make plans and carry them out? Or are the plans realistic? Are they forever making plans that they can not execute? Maybe we are getting too far afield from "personhood."

BJB: From personhood, which is the overarching "P."

JM: From personhood. Right.

I guess that is the question: what are the interpersonal processes that enliven the personhood of your client?

BJB: Yes.

JM: And, if you will, we know to be true to enliven *our* person-hood–so the client has got a person to relate to.

WHAT ARE THE LONGINGS?
WHAT ARE THE CHALLENGES?

BJB: Thinking of one I have got to see this afternoon. Last week was *so* attacking and I am trying to think, "What is the thing in here?"

JM: What gets in the way or what does she throw up to keep you and herself isolated?

BJB: My personhood door tends to slam shut after much of an attack. I am not good at it.

JM: What is she attacking you about?

BJB: Oh, I don't know–I'm her mother.

JM: Uh huh. Were you the good mother to begin with?

BJB: Sometimes. The day before I had been.

JM: Well, I think that is a good question. How do we keep our hearts open while our clients are flailing around in their blaming, agitated, condescending, and sometimes, intimidating ways?

BJB: Right. How do you do that?

JM: I think, at one level, I would say it is kind of like an aikido process: I am not absorbing. I am letting that move on off. Like I am diverting. I am diverting the blame energy. And I try to keep open and interested to hear about the person's pain–which I know is theirs and was theirs before they ever met me. So, in a sense, this attack on me–it could be looked at–it is just like a narrative that is happening on somebody's family map.

So what is the issue here for this person? What is the longing? What is the challenge? Try to stay focused on her. Keep being in touch with my breathing. That is one of the ways. Thank God for Virginia's teaching me about that one. Because, literally, if I bring my awareness back to my breathing and just try to keep my breathing open and easy, I can take in more. But I don't–I am really looking for a way to not get distracted or disconnected from the person. Because that is what they are skilled at. It is in their time of pain or, in their time of this-didn't-work-right or that-didn't-work-right, that they learned that the connection could not be sustained.

This woman sounds very difficult. She travels emotionally over vast territories. So just keeping up with where she is really coming from, I would think, would be hard.

BJB: That is probably the key problem.

JM: What do you mean?

BJB: I had no *idea* she was going to come in that day in that frame. I was just absolutely caught off guard with it. But she does it frequently. Or often enough that it is not something that does not happen.

JM: So today she might come in and be in a much more collaborative mode?

BJB: Quite possible. Even be apologetic. Or she might not keep the appointment. She swore she wasn't coming. Either one just as likely.

JM: Well, how do *you* do it?

BJB: How do I do it? *When* I do it–I sometimes do not manage to do it–but, *when* I do it, it is by being able to see the desperate child.

JM: Um hmm.

BJB: Somehow or another that does not necessarily work even if I do.

JM: Right. But I think that is a huge one, for me, too. To know and sense that little girl or that little boy. I think the trick, for me–Carol and I were having a conversation last night–she is reading an interesting book called, *In Session,* on transformation. New book, really sounds good. Was it Schiff (1975) who used to take the people in and re-parent them? [Carol] says, "Jean, you do this inner child thing and then sometimes you have these little stuffed critters for these people. I do not understand why you do that." I was saying, "Well, I am wanting people to–I use it as a "visual aid," a kinesthetic aid, an auditory-sensory aid–to help people acknowledge that they have got this little girl or little boy that still lives inside them.

I think the way I am able to work with people as disturbed as they are and still take long periods of time off and not have–not be harassed at home by telephone calls and all–I do not become the parent to that little child, I am constantly working for them to accept that they now have to learn to parent that little child. And so I am wanting–I am in a sense almost using the adult as my co-therapist to help that little one–to help the little one inside.

So I don't know whether this woman you are talking about–perhaps she keeps trying to put the little one in *your* lap.

BJB: She has got this dynamic that goes on that she gets *mad* at the thought that she has got to be the one who does this.

JM: Well, I can't blame her! That is bad enough–why you have to do it . . . because, too, if you found your loved one–if you found the one you really loved–then *they* were going to do it. If your parents didn't do it, then you get the second chance. Your lover is going to do it.

Well [the heck with] that one too. That little Jean, she keeps coming back to me. I am stuck with her. As I have come to appreciate this, she does not want anybody else really. She wants *my* acceptance. She wants me to really value her experience, her feelings, her needs. And there is no other part of me that turns me into my basic needs faster, than to think about little Jean. She is the wisest one about our emotional needs. Maybe our spiritual needs, too.

BJB: Um hmm.

JM: So that is a part about tapping into the personhood–our own as well as our client's. Is really appreciating the–I do not want to say the "little girl" or the "little boy inside"–but that is what it is. That is the best metaphor I know to help people appreciate their vulnerabilities, their real human-ness. Adults, we have learned to be so machine-like.

BJB: I know.

JM: Anyway, you must have done your job mighty good because I have just been rattling. I have enjoyed talking and having time with you, appreciating your being willing to get this on tape.

NOTE

1. Pain, pleasure, plans, problems, performance, and power.

REFERENCES

McLendon, J. (1996). The Tao of communication and the constancy of change, in B.J. Brothers (Ed.), *Couples and the Tao of Congruence*. Binghamton, New York: The Haworth Press, Inc., 35-49.

McLendon, J. (1998, May/June) Healing the ailing workplace. *IEEE Software: Journal for the International Electrical Electronics Engineers Computer Society.* 97-99.

Schiff, J.L. (1975). *The cathexis reader.* New York, Evanston, San Francisco, London: Harper & Row.

Personhood of the Therapist
in Couples Therapy:
An Integrity Therapy Perspective

Nedra R. Lander
Danielle Nahon

SUMMARY. Integrity Therapy (Lander, 1986; Lander & Nahon, 1992a, 1995a; Mowrer, 1961b, 1964a) views the personhood of the therapist as the very essence of therapy. By meeting the deepest part of the therapist with the deepest self of individuals in therapy, a healing process unfolds which opens up the healing potential of both the individuals and the couple. This article offers couple therapists and other mental health professionals an Integrity Therapy perspective of the personhood of the therapist and its therapeutic potential for helping couples in distress to reclaim their personhood. Two aspects of the Integrity Therapy approach which play a critical role in enhancing therapists' use of their personhood in the therapeutic process are explored: (a) the use

Nedra R. Lander is affiliated with Civic Site, Ottawa Hospital, Ottawa, Ontario, Canada and the Faculty of Medicine, University of Ottawa, Ottawa, Ontario, Canada.

Danielle Nahon is affiliated with the Faculty of Medicine, University of Ottawa, and the Corporation for Research and Education on Gender, Health and Multicultural Issues International, Nepean, Canada.

The authors would like to thank their partners–Stephen J. West for his help as their copy editor, and Stephen and Emil Lander for their support and gift of time. Finally, the authors would like to thank Ed Barton for his encouragement to share their tradecraft with others.

Address correspondence to: Dr. Nedra Lander, Department of Psychiatry, CPC 3, Civic Site, Ottawa Hospital, 1053 Carling Avenue, Ottawa, Ontario, Canada K1Y 4E9.

[Haworth co-indexing entry note]: "Personhood of the Therapist in Couples Therapy: An Integrity Therapy Perspective." Lander, Nedra R., and Danielle Nahon. Co-published simultaneously in *Journal of Couples Therapy* (The Haworth Press, Inc.) Vol. 9, No. 3/4, 2000, pp. 29-42; and: *The Personhood of the Therapist* (ed: Barbara Jo Brothers) The Haworth Press, Inc., 2000, pp. 29-42. Single or multiple copies of this article are available for a fee from The Haworth Document Delivery Service [1-800-342-9678, 9:00 a.m. - 5:00 p.m. (EST). E-mail address: getinfo@haworthpressinc.com].

of therapist self-disclosure, and (b) therapists' awareness and therapeutic use of counter-transference issues. *[Article copies available for a fee from The Haworth Document Delivery Service: 1-800-342-9678. E-mail address: <getinfo@haworthpressinc.com> Website: <http://www.HaworthPress.com>]*

KEYWORDS. Psychotherapy, counselling, couple therapy, Integrity Therapy, counter-transference, therapist-client relationship, humanistic, existential, family therapy, counselling relationship

All therapeutic approaches claim to focus on the role of the therapist as a key variable in predicting positive therapeutic outcome. Integrity Therapy (Lander, 1986; Lander & Mowrer (1969-73); Lander & Nahon, 1986, 1988a, 1992a, 1995a; Mowrer, 1953, 1961a, 1964a, 1976) begun by O. H. Mowrer in the 1930's–an existential model which views mental illness as stemming from a lack of fidelity to one's value system–views the therapist's personhood as the very essence of therapy. By meeting the deepest part of the therapist with the deepest self of individuals in therapy, a healing process unfolds which opens up the healing potential of both the individuals and the couple. From the Integrity Therapy perspective, the personhood of the therapist is emphasized not only regardless of or in addition to the treatment philosophy, but rather as the very core of the treatment philosophy. Two major aspects of the Integrity Therapy approach play a critical role in enhancing therapists' use of their personhood in the therapeutic process: (a) the encouragement of therapist self-disclosure, and (b) the therapist's awareness and therapeutic use of counter-transference issues.

The objective of this article is to offer couple therapists and other mental health professionals an Integrity Therapy perspective on the personhood of the therapist, its enhancement and its therapeutic potential for helping couples in distress. Our aim is to share therapeutic tradecraft as to the manner in which the Integrity Therapy approach allows therapists to use their own selves as a therapeutic medium in helping couples own their accessible potential for transcending their personal tragedies, traumas and relationship challenges.

INTEGRITY THERAPY: PHILOSOPHICAL PERSPECTIVE

Integrity Therapy is an existential therapeutic framework in terms of both substance and form. The existential framework aims to clarify, reflect upon and understand life, focussing on the process of living (van Deurzen-Smith, 1988) and the uniqueness of individuals, their values, and the search for meaning in their lives (Coleman, 1976). Following its existential basis, a major assumption underlying Integrity Therapy is that the human being has the capacity to choose between good and evil (Lander & Nahon, 1989; Lowe, 1969), and that truth is subjective and that the discovery of truth comprises a major life goal for human beings (Lander & Nahon, in press). Integrity Therapy views the process of therapy as being unique to each individual and to each context, and thus as one which cannot be "manualized"–in other words, cannot be presented in a cookbook approach. Also, there is no "integrity-speak." We use words and metaphors of the individuals in therapy, because it is their voice, rather than that of therapist or of theory, which needs to be heard. Contrary to tradition, we do not utilize the case study format, as in our view, no case study can truly capture the essence of a human encounter. What is not revealed is the context, the demand characteristics and the non-verbal interactions within the therapeutic encounter. Consequently, all the tenets of integrity are violated. The resulting interaction is a barren one in which the other is left seeking out another therapeutic experience in order to bridge the existential void which has been created.

The reader will notice that the usual terms of "client" and "patient" are absent from this article. Mowrer viewed the human being as a valuing animal, with a profound need to have a sense of connection and community with others (Mowrer, 1961a, 1964a). Consequently, he emphasized the importance of the Latin word "relegare," translated as religion and connection. We feel that to refer to individuals as either patients or clients perpetuates a sense of hierarchical split and professional narcissism which is too prevalent in the professional literature. Inherent in this hierarchical structure is the safety of distance from the other which implies a greater health or personal integration. In contrast, Integrity Therapy views all human beings as being somewhere along the road to recovery. Our references to the consumer or recipient of therapeutic services as the person or individual in therapy reflects a relationship between two equal human beings, along the lines of what Martin Buber refers to an "I-Thou" rather than an "I-It" relationship (Buber, 1970). As a deliberate choice on their part, the authors will thus honour "relegare"–a pivotal tenet of Integrity Therapy–in this article through the use of their first names, by establishing a more personal connection with the reader and keeping connected to the triad of mind, body and soul which is essential to Integrity Therapy.

Integrity Therapy stresses equality of the couple (or individual) in therapy to the therapist, and the couple's role in the therapeutic process (Lander & Nahon, 1992b, 1995b). The process of change in therapy is seen as being the task and responsibility of the couple, rather than that of the therapist. From the Integrity Therapy framework, the therapist does not guide the couple. Rather, the couple takes the lead and the therapist follows (Lander & Nahon, 1988b).

INTEGRITY THERAPY: THEORETICAL UNDERPINNINGS

Integrity Therapy views mental illness as resulting from a personal lack of integrity with self and others (Lander & Nahon, 1988a, 1988b; Mowrer, 1961a). Integrity is operationally defined as comprising three necessary elements: honesty, responsibility, and increased emotional involvement with others (Mowrer, 1964a; Mowrer & Vattano, 1976), also known as closure of the emotional space with others (Lander & Nahon, 1995b), which are defined as follows:

Honesty means being open and truthful about one's feelings, attitudes and actions–past, present and future. It involves acknowledging past or present wrong-doings which may have caused problems in one's life or another's life. It means being willing to own 100% of one's 50% in contributing to a dysfunctional interaction with others as the first step in resolving the conflict. In dealing with a personal or interpersonal transgression, this type of honesty becomes critical. After a person has been radically honest within a relationship, a strange and wondrous experience begins to take place: one finds that the very secrets hidden in fear of rejection from others have instead helped to draw others close. One discovers that past defensive behaviours and facades are no longer necessary and that one can relax, be oneself and begin to work on problems as they now exist.

Responsibility means making amends or setting things right once the acknowledgement of wrong-doing has been made. According to Mowrer (personal communication, 1970), it is not enough "to dump one's garbage"; one must then do something about it. A person who has "gotten into a mess" must assume the responsibility for getting out of it. This approach, integrated with the honest accountability for one's transgressions, again goes a long way towards ensuring that the other(s) in a conflictual situation will be willing to listen. When one individual has been willing to become responsible to the other in this manner, the other will more often than not come forward non-defensively and risk becoming accountable and responsible in return.

Community or increased emotional involvement with others is perhaps the most unique component of integrity, as it is so rarely a natural ingredient of most human interactions. Emotional involvement requires that the ultimate intent of a conflict-resolution, or for that matter, of any meaningful interpersonal interaction, be one of "closing the psychological space" between two or more individuals, or in other words, increasing one's sense of community with the others (Lander & Nahon, 1992a).

THE PERSONHOOD OF THE THERAPIST: THERAPIST SELF-DISCLOSURE

Mowrer was an adviser to Alcoholics Anonymous (AA) and other twelve-step programs including Day Top Village and Synanon. Consequently, AA and many of the related Twelve-step based programs bear a strong conceptual link with the principles of the Integrity Therapy Model (Lander & Nahon, 1996). Mowrer's work was thus the first to stress the therapeutic value of therapist self-disclosure (Mowrer, 1964b) and this has been further carried out by Lander (1986) and Lander and Nahon (1988b, 1992a, 1995a). We believe that the traditional proscribed therapists' secretiveness or neutrality denies the human relationship which they aim to foster, thereby limiting their effectiveness. Consequently, we encourage therapists, when they are comfortable to do so, to share their past misdeeds and their present struggles to behave with scrupulous integrity. This atmosphere encourages the development of meaningful human relationships with others which allows for the transcendence of disabling problems. To quote Mowrer, "it seems that it is the truth spoken rather than the treatment one receives that heals" (personal communication, 1969).

The therapist's willingness to self-disclose lessens the possibility of an authority battle with couples in therapy (Lander & Nahon, 1996). The Integrity approach in couple therapy encourages a seeking of counsel rather than a seeking or giving of advice by anyone including the therapist. This avoids the image of the wheel in which everything is connected through the hub of the leader, thus keeping the circle from being broken. Resistances in the couple are seen as an unwillingness for everyone to hold themselves accountable or to be responsible for the problems of living. As couples challenge these resistances by calling into question each other's excuses, one is not obliged to accept the considerations offered. Rather, one is asked to listen and then make one's own decision. Thus couples in therapy cannot hold the therapist, each other or others responsible for choices made. For example, we are both outraged when we hear from couples in therapy that former therapists encouraged or even outright told them to leave their spouse; in so doing, therapists allowed the couple to escape responsibility for their decisions.

When based on the assumption that the therapist will be responsible for bailing one out, the view of therapy as a seeking of counsel discourages unilateral decision-making. A major tenet of Integrity Therapy is that people get into emotional difficulties because they are not living up to their own values–i.e., that they are violating the contracts and commitments which they themselves have made (Lander & Nahon, 1992b), even with themselves. Ultimately, the judgement of whether or not one has honoured one's own value system is a personal one, sidestepping the potential control battles with others which may be seen as resistance.

Nedra and Danielle have differing approaches to self-disclosure, based in part on the differing needs of the populations of individuals with whom they work as well as personal values. Their differing approaches towards therapist self-disclosure underline that there is no cookbook formula for self-disclosure in Integrity Therapy. Rather, what is most critical is that therapists be consistent in their level of self-disclosure (Nahon & Lander, 1992). Nedra's approach towards self-disclosure is that she offers at the pre-commitment interview a brief and discreet (yet integritous) outline of her life, personal issues and crises, values and biases, as well as what she views to be her major defence patterns. With couples, she talks about her work in sharing space and power with her husband Emil. For example, she shares her own creative challenges and struggles to share space in decorating, combining her love for Victorian clutter with her husband Emil's minimalist preferences, or to live harmoniously with a day bird while being herself a committed night owl. She speaks poignantly of how when she was first married to Emil, she took up his offer to do the dishes. However, she came to realize that there was no integrity in expecting him to do the dishes on her time schedule and not his, and that if she was going to delegate, she realized it really meant delegating the power to carry out this task according to his own rhythm. She thus decided that there was more integrity in taking over the dishes again, and honouring her own values as to time boundaries for getting this done.

Danielle's self-disclosure in therapy is less systematic. First, given the briefer nature of her therapeutic work, there is no pre-commitment interview as such. Rather, she presents the first session in therapy as being an evaluative or "mutual eyeballing" one for both individuals. Thus individuals can enter therapy with a much greater sense of power inherent in the ability to be able to make a choice themselves as to whether or not there is a sense of fit and comfort in working with her. Within the therapeutic relationship, Danielle engages in self-disclosure depending on her level of comfort and what she sees as the appropriateness and fit within a given situation. She discloses some of her values which she feels are particularly relevant to a harmonious working relationship in therapy–for example, her discomfort with violence as a viable means for expressing one's feelings, her religious values, and her likes or dislikes for particular communication styles in herself and others. She always begins her discussion of Integrity Therapy by stating that she finds this model to be helpful to her in as part of her own journey of soul-searching and self-exploration. Her level of and comfort with self-disclosure has increased dramatically over time. She sees this as a function of her own personal evolution as a human being and of her continuing professional development within the practice of Integrity Therapy.

With couples, she shares a great deal about her own couple relationship and how she finds that the Integrity Therapy perspective helps her with closing space, dealing with those daily "little" things that she feels make or break a relationship, dealing with conflicts and closing the space when angry, as well as dealing with what she sees as challenges arising from reciprocal negative counter-transferences. Couples in therapy find these disclosures quite helpful, in that they offer a model for a daily challenge to behave with integrity, and they dispel the myths that the therapist has it all together, and that healthy relationships should happen automatically and without continuously committed hard work.

If therapists are uncomfortable about or unwilling to self-disclose, for example due to personality, personal preference and values, or therapeutic model, this non-disclosure is viable as long as it is openly owned and made a part of the explicit or implicit therapeutic contract. As we indicated (Nahon & Lander, 1992), a lack of disclosure on the part of the therapist is less problematic than inconsistent disclosure. If the therapist initially self-discloses and then withdraws from the other, this often leads to a sense of rejection and betrayal by the other. It is then the lack of integrity, not the lack of disclosure which is the problem. A caveat for therapists regarding self-disclosure in therapy is that revealing one's personhood is also an explicit invitation to self-exploration as may be requested by the other.

Therapists attending our workshops often ask "Isn't therapist self-disclosure destructive? Does it not lead to a diffusion of boundaries between therapist and client?" In our view, therapist self-disclosure is only destructive if it is misused–in other words, if it is used without integrity, i.e., lacking in honesty, responsibility, or community. In our view, therapist self-disclosure–if engaged in with scrupulous integrity–is both positive and therapeutic in that it allows individuals in therapy to articulate and clarify their own values in differentiating the "like me" and the "not like me" from the clearly articulated self and boundaries of the therapist. Nothing grows in a vacuum. In fact, the reason that children and adolescents respond so well to boundaries defined by clear and consistent messages is that these boundaries offer them a sense of security. This in turn enables them to decide more clearly whether given types of behaviours and their consequences are acceptable within their value systems. When parents abandon adolescents as being adult and thus no longer feel that it is worth the inconvenience of organizing their lives around them, adolescents act out. At some level, their goal is to mobilize their parents to reappear and take action and to define themselves by the relational encounter with their parents. Only then can they afford to get on with the task of individuating from their parents, often by actively ignoring them. Similarly with couples, there is a sense of security which arises from knowing where the other is, and what the values and boundaries of the other are, so as to help clarify one's boundaries and values.

Our willingness to share own our fears, insecurities and basic human foibles with couples in therapy seems critical in helping them to transcend their profound sense of inherent defect and their desperate

striving towards unattainable goals. Sometimes, in spite of themselves, these individuals and couples begin to shift from viewing their
symptoms as insurmountable towards beginning to see them as acceptable and even creative warning signals which are activated whenever they committed a personal transgression. By stressing our own
authenticity, we communicate our respect for these individuals'
unique capacity for self-expression and self-transcendence. Furthermore, as we self-disclose these individuals and couples begin to understand that inherent in their own vulnerability is their greatest
strength. Consequently, the challenges of sharing space and of respecting the boundaries and values of the other, are able to be integrated on
a much deeper cognitive and emotional level, as the individuals and
the couple reclaim their personhood.

PERSONHOOD OF THE THERAPIST
AND COUNTER-TRANSFERENCE

In an earlier publication in this journal (Lander & Nahon, 1995a),
we suggested that in order to deal viably with counter-transference,
therapists must constantly be vigilant of the underlying issues which
may occur within the therapeutic encounter. In order to do this, therapists must engage in an ongoing process of scrupulous honesty and
self-examination. Within the context of couple therapy, the risks of
counter-transference become exponentially increased because of the
triadic nature of the relationship. We indicate, however, that far too
often, therapists use the jargon label of counter-transference in a manner which protects them from truly owning their conflictual feelings
towards the couple.

We believe that the therapist does not represent or symbolize significant others. Rather, the therapist is a significant other, and the quality
of the therapist/other relationship is not symbolic but real. Therapists
must own their dark side and be willing to be accountable and responsible for it (Lander & Nahon, in press). It is vital for the therapist to
deal in complete integrity with the confrontations regarding the therapist's foibles, personality quirks, and possible slips within the therapeutic relationship. This has a dramatic impact in equalizing the power
differential between both individuals. Each is now fully accountable
and responsible for personal contributions to the relationship (Lander &

Nahon, 1995a, 1995b), and therefore able to fully own their person-hood.

In the course of treatment, we as therapists sometimes face another interesting form of counter-transference. This occurs when those individuals with whom we have trouble working remind us of our own selves at an earlier developmental stage which had less integrity. In Jungian terms, it is as though these individuals comprise our "shadow"–in other words, those parts of the self which are disowned, and thus follow behind us like a shadow (Nahon & Lander, 1994). If we are to reclaim our personhood, we must own our shadows. The challenge for us as therapists in dealing with this relational issue is to own our historical–and often less integritous–selves, to validate the distance travelled, to reaffirm the boundary between old self and new self, and to resist the seductive allure to engage in old destructive patterns of relating. In so doing, we are challenged to behave with integrity within the therapeutic relationship and in our own personal lives. By acknowledging that we too are on the road to recovery, we as therapists reach a higher plane of integrity and authenticity, truly being able to speak with the voice of "walking the talk" (Mowrer, personal communication, 1969).

DISCUSSION

Integrity Therapy offers a novel approach towards enhancing the personhood of couple therapists, and the creative use of their selves as a viable medium for positive therapeutic change within the couple. A re-conceptualization of therapist self-disclosure challenges traditional therapeutic approaches which often discourage therapist self-disclosure based on the concern that if one were to do so, therapists might either lose their credibility, or even worse, interfere with the transferential relationship. From the Integrity perspective, therapist self-disclosure results in a positive qualitative shift in the power distribution between therapist and couple. It allows the therapist to credibly challenge the behaviour of the individuals in therapy–and vice-versa–from the position of an equal. In this regard, Mowrer's phrase, now popularized in the self-help movements is apropos: "you can only talk the talk if you have walked the walk" (personal communication, 1969).

Mowrer also often spoke of the lack of integrity inherent in asking individuals in therapy to do something that therapists were not willing to do themselves–for example, to self-disclose and self-explore. In couple work, the disclosures of therapists' own self-work in their personal relationships provides a model for the couple. Furthermore, and even more importantly, it challenges the myth, commonly held as a belief by many individuals in therapy, that the therapists' own lives and relationships are perfect. As therapists are able to share the struggle to share space within their own relationships, to maintain a sense of self within the relationship, to use their personal power to nurture romance, and to dare and grow with another human being as two lives converge into an ever synergistic and creative partnership, this provides the couple in therapy with a sense of hope which mobilizes their potential for positive repair work and healing of their selves and of the couple.

Furthermore, from our experience, it is much more therapeutic for therapists to clearly draw a boundary by declaring their values and boundaries regarding what are acceptable versus unacceptable behaviours in their own value system; it provides couples in therapy with a real relationship, where they can dare to articulate and differentiate their own value systems. Who we are is fundamentally what our values are, and what our counter-transferences are. Often, the concept of counter-transference is compartmentalised into being either positive or negative to therapy. In fact, we view all relationships–and in particular couple relationships–as being counter-transferential in nature. Couple work is really an exponential or factorial effect of individual counter-transferences and their dyadic pairings and counter-pairings. With such chaotic potential, it is essential for someone in the therapeutic relationship to have some grounding by knowing their counter-transferential issues and to have the courage to make them an overt part of the therapeutic process and the therapeutic relationship.

Self-knowledge and comfort with the self is thus a cornerstone of the Integrity Therapy model. We see the therapeutic use of counter-transference to be a critical component in the therapist's use of self as a therapeutic agent of change. This leads us to the conclusion that if counter-transference is not carefully owned and used by therapists within the therapeutic relationship, this will diminish their true personhood, and thus of their potential therapeutic effectiveness.

In our work with numerous couples labelled as difficult or untreatable, there is little acting out and the drop-out rate is very low. It would seem that the validity given to the therapeutic alliance as a bona fide relationship and our own striving to be real at all times minimizes the need for these couples to act out. The therapeutic success of these couples has reaffirmed our faith in the capacity of all human beings–however seemingly hopeless–to transcend their pathology and find a sense of joy and meaning in their existence. Our observations point to the dichotomy of professionalism versus humanity as a pivotal therapeutic dilemma. It is the issue of therapist as a person versus therapist as an armamentarium of techniques which poke, manipulate and manoeuvre. This dichotomy is firmly rooted in our Western rationalist view of science, whereby in order to study a phenomenon, one must become distanciated and hence non-involved. To transcend this requires tremendous personal courage. In many ways it is not at all different from the tremendously difficult task that we ask of individuals and couples in therapy whom we challenge to transcend their pathologies.

We have repeatedly observed this struggle, often in a helpless fashion, amongst training therapists who waver between the security of time-honoured and sanctioned modes of behaviour versus the forbidden temptation to break all of the rules and become real. How ironic it is that of all professions, we in the mental health and care-giving professions–who aspire to kindle the flame of human spirit in others–have become seduced by the idea that to be a professional means to wear a mask of neutrality with its implied superiority over another, and thereby to squelch one's own spark of humanness. And yet, to paraphrase the lessons learnt by the hero of a favourite children's story, "The Velveteen Rabbit," love means getting your hair messed up, love means you risk getting hurt, and yet only love can make you real (Williams, 1975). Perhaps one can only unlock the healing potential of couples in therapy through a real human encounter, daring to nakedly meet the other on equal terms. Only then can that ever-elusive therapeutic magic occur, the magic of reclaiming one's personhood and becoming real.

REFERENCES

Buber, M. (1970). *I and thou.* New York: Charles Scribner's Sons.

Coleman, J.C. (1976). *Abnormal psychology and modern life.* Glenview: Scott, Foresman & Co.

Lander, N.R. (1986, October). *Hobart Mowrer's Integrity (Therapy) groups.* Paper presented at the annual meeting of the Canadian Group Psychotherapy Association, Gray Rocks, Québec, 1986.

Lander, N.R., & Mowrer, O.H. (1969-1973). *Group Co-Leadership of Integrity Community Groups.* Urbana, IL.

Lander, N.R., & Nahon, D. (1986). *Treating the "untreatable" patient: A case study in unlabelling.* Paper presented at the American Psychological Association Annual meeting, Washington, DC.

Lander, N.R., & Nahon, D. (1988a, August) *Mowrer's integrity therapy: An old concept revisited.* Paper presented at the American Psychological Association Annual meeting, Atlanta, Georgia.

Lander, N.R., & Nahon, D. (1988b, August). *Integrity therapy: A vision for the nineties.* Paper presented at the XXIVth International Congress of Psychology, Sydney, Australia.

Lander, N.R., & Nahon, D. (1989, August). *Values of the therapist: Reformulating the therapeutic impasse.* Paper presented at the American Psychological Association annual meeting, New Orleans, Louisiana.

Lander, N.R. & Nahon, D. (1992a). Betrayed within the therapeutic relationship: An Integrity Therapy perspective. *The Psychotherapy Patient, 8* (3-4), 113-126.

Lander, N.R. & Nahon, D. (1992b). Betrayed within the therapeutic relationship: An Integrity Therapy perspective. In Stern, E.M., *Betrayal in psychotherapy and its antidotes: Challenges for patient and therapist* (pp. 113-125). New York: The Haworth Press, Inc.

Lander, N.R., & Nahon, D. (1995a). Danger or opportunity: Countertransference in couples therapy from an Integrity Therapy perspective. *Journal of Couples Therapy, 5*(3), 72-92.

Lander, N.R., & Nahon, D. (1995b). Danger or opportunity: Countertransference in couples therapy from an Integrity Therapy perspective. In Brothers, B.J. (Ed.), *Couples and countertransference* (pp. 72-92). Binghamton: The Haworth Press, Inc.

Lander, N.R. & Nahon, D. (1996, October). *Impasses within the group: Issues of values and therapist integrity.* Paper presented at the annual meeting of the Canadian Group Psychotherapy Association, Ottawa, Ontario.

Lander, N.R., & Nahon, D. (in press). Working with Men from a Mythopoetic Perspective: An Integrity Therapy Framework. In Barton, E. (Ed.), Mythopoetic Perspective of Men's Healing Work for Therapists and Others. Greenwood: East Lansing, MI.

Lowe, C.M. (1969). *Value orientations in counseling and psychotherapy.* San Francisco: Chandler.

Mowrer, O.H. (1953). *Psychotherapy: Theory and research.* New York: The Ronald Press.

Mowrer, O.H. (1961a). *The crisis in psychiatry and religion.* Princeton, NJ: D. Van Nostrand.

Mowrer, O.H. (1961b). The rediscovery of responsibility. *Special Supplement on Psychiatry in American Life, Atlantic Monthly, 7,* 88-91.

Mowrer, O.H. (1964a). *The new group therapy.* Princeton, NJ: D. Van Nostrand.

Mowrer, O.H. (1964b). Freudianism, behaviour therapy and "self-disclosure." *Behaviour Research & Therapy, 1,* 321-337.

Mowrer, O.H. (1976). Changing conceptions of neurosis and the small-groups movement. *Education, 97*(1), 24-62.

Mowrer, O.H., & Vattano, A.J. (1976). Integrity groups: A context for growth in honesty, responsibility, and involvement. *Journal of Applied Behavioral Science, 12*(3), 419-431.

Nahon, D., & Lander, N.R. (1992). A clinic for men: Challenging individual and social myths. *Journal of Mental Health Counseling, 14*, 405-416.

Nahon, D. & Lander, N.R. (1994, June). *Widening the Circle: The Men's Clinic, Life Force and Metamorphosis*. Plenary presentation at the 1994 Conference on Men and Health Care, University of Alberta, Edmonton, Alberta.

van Deurzen-Smith, E. (1988). *Existential Counselling in practice*. London: Sage.

Williams, M. (1975). *The velveteen rabbit or how toys become real*. New York: Avon Books.

Toward the Meaning
of "The Person of the Therapist"

Edward W. L. Smith

SUMMARY. Too often, in discussions of psychotherapy, the techniques are given undue emphasis. Research suggests that the same techniques are differentially effective when used by equally trained and supervised therapists. Not only are some therapists more effective, irrespective of the type of therapy they practice, but some, because of their personal qualities, may actually harm those with whom they work. This research reflects the vast importance of the ubiquitous element in therapy, that of the "person" of the therapist. The question, then, follows, how may personhood be developed? This question is explored as it relates to both breadth and depth of life experience. *[Article copies available for a fee from The Haworth Document Delivery Service: 1-800-342-9678. E-mail address: <getinfo@haworthpressinc.com> Website: <http://www.HaworthPress.com>]*

KEYWORDS. Psychotherapy, "person" of the therapist, personal growth, personhood

Intrigued by a certain mystique which attended it, I was drawn to membership in the American Academy of Psychotherapists in the

Edward W. L. Smith, PhD, is Professor of Psychology and Coordinator of Clinical Training, Georgia Southern University. He has published six books, his most recent (co-edited), being *Touch in Psychotherapy: Theory, Research, and Practice.* A Diplomate of the American Board of Professional Psychology (ABPP), he is a long time member of the editorial board of the *Journal of Couples Therapy.*

[Haworth co-indexing entry note]: "Toward the Meaning of 'The Person of the Therapist.'" Smith, Edward W. L. Co-published simultaneously in *Journal of Couples Therapy* (The Haworth Press, Inc.) Vol. 9, No. 3/4, 2000, pp. 43-49; and: *The Personhood of the Therapist* (ed: Barbara Jo Brothers) The Haworth Press, Inc., 2000, pp. 43-49. Single or multiple copies of this article are available for a fee from The Haworth Document Delivery Service [1-800-342-9678, 9:00 a.m. - 5:00 p.m. (EST). E-mail address: getinfo@haworthpressinc.com].

early 1970s. That mystique was, for me, summarized and at the same time enhanced by the credo which I heard–"The Academy is dedicated to the continued development of the person of the therapist." This concept fascinated me and my fascination was increased by the odd phrasing, "the person of the therapist." This phrase begs expatiation, so to that end I offer what follows.

One has only to read the psychotherapy research reported and summarized during the decade of the nineties to conclude that psychotherapy is, in general, effective. (For quick and easy reference, see the Lambert and Bergin [1994] chapter on "The effectiveness of Psychotherapy.") But too often, perhaps, we tend to overemphasize the techniques, the procedures, the methods. In fact, it is by its techniques, oftentimes, that a therapeutic system is most readily identified. This is a simplification which loses the richness of understanding afforded only when the philosophical underpinnings and the whole body of theory–developmental theory, theory of natural personality functioning, theory of psychopathology, theory of psychotherapy–are considered.

But beyond the philosophy, the theory, and the body of techniques, there is something more, something of a different plane. Techniques, as well as philosophies and theories, are abstractions. As abstractions, techniques are made concrete only through the work of the therapist. That is, technique is given life through the person of the therapist. The technique only becomes a lived event as it is brought to life through the therapist's personal expression.

In the words of Lambert and Bergin (1994, p. 167), "The complexity and subtlety of psychotherapeutic processes cannot be reduced to a set of disembodied techniques because techniques gain their meaning and, in turn, their effectiveness from the particular interaction of the individuals involved." With their characteristic attention to research evidence, they report that " . . . despite careful selection, training, monitoring, and supervision, therapists offering the same treatments can have highly divergent results" (Lambert & Bergin, 1994, p. 174). The conclusion to be drawn, then, is that the same techniques have differential effectiveness through the personal expressions of equally trained and supervised therapists! Lambert and Bergin (1994, p. 182) go on to state that "The therapist factor, as a contributor to outcome, is looming large in the assessment of outcomes." Furthermore, based on compelling evidence, a portion of those whom therapy " . . . is intended to help are actually harmed by . . . negative therapist character-istics," among other factors (Lambert & Bergin, 1994, p. 182).

Perhaps it would be good to emphasize, here, that "The individual therapist can play a surprisingly large role in treatment outcome even when treatment is being offered within the stipulations of manual-guided therapy" (Lambert & Bergin, 1994, p. 181). So, even when therapy is done "by the book," as verified through training, supervision, and monitoring, different therapists evidence different levels of effectiveness.

The intriguing conclusion which Lambert and Bergin (1994, p. 181) draw from their review of the relevant research is " . . . that training programs should emphasize the *development of the therapist as a person* in parity with the acquisition of therapeutic techniques" (italics mine).

It may be interesting to consider the placement of different psycho-therapies on a continuum of relationship and techniquefulness. At one pole would be found the approach developed by the early Atlanta Psychiatric Clinic (Felder, Malone, Warkentin, Whitaker), Helmuth Kaiser, and some of the experiential therapies. The antipole would represent behavior therapy. In its extremity, the former pole could be summarized by the belief that "relationship is everything." The anti-pole, then, could be summarized as "technique is everything."

These antipodes are perhaps a bit forced, but do call attention to the fact that therapists of various theoretical persuasions disagree as to the relative importance of personhoods interacting or technical manipula-tions. One would have us believe that it is relationship, the other that it is technique alone which carries the day. With respect to personhood, obviously those at the pole of relationship would embrace the belief in its importance. Those at the antipode may need reminder of the re-search evidence concerning the importance of personal qualities in therapy outcome. Most therapies fall somewhere between the antipodes and reveal the fact that no matter what the therapy, there cannot be disembodied technique in the consulting room, nor can there be a therapist present who does not fill the time and space with her or his presence.

And, now, for the crux of the matter. What is "the person of the therapist?"

Irma Lee Shepard (1992) has expressed doubt that psychotherapy can be taught, just as being an artist cannot be taught. It is personal resources which are crucial and must be developed in order for a therapist to transcend artificially applied techniques. Shepard (1992, p. 239) calls forth the "power and authenticity of the person" as that which is needed for one to *be* a therapist and not just *do* therapy.

Growth in personhood accrues, I believe, through experience under conditions of heightened awareness. But to appreciate this, we must first understand both the meaning of the term "experience" and the term "heightened awareness."

"Experience" derives from the Latin *experiri,* meaning "to try, to test." Through its Latin root, "experience" is etymologically related to the word "experiment." By "experience," then, is meant trying things out, testing things, finding out about the world and about one-self in the world. As one experiments more with the world, with life, one gains in knowledge and in understanding. As knowledge and understanding accrue, one can account for more and more of that to which one is exposed. Such knowing of things and about things and understanding of the relationships among things accumulates with continued trying and testing. But such accumulation is not limited to the realm of thought or idea. It involves the realm of feeling or emo-tional learning and the realm of action. Aristotle acknowledged these three as the realms of human experience–cognition, affect, conation.

Considering experience, then, as cognitive, affective and conative we begin to appreciate the meaning of breadth of experience. To have broad experience implicates all of the realms of experience and also implies a wide range of exposure to life and the world. Such a view was captured by Michael Adam (1976, p. 18) when he stated that Hindus believed that " . . . a man should grow to maturity by way of experiences that left no dark corners in him, no 'unlived lives.'" Wide exposure is implicated.

Yet, exposure to some things seems richer than exposure to certain other things. In his explication of a humanistic ethic, James Bugenthal (1971) listed as one of its points a commitment to growth-oriented experiencing. Here is evidence of a recognition that some types of experiencing are richer in the sense that they hold higher potential for growth. Perhaps only the individual, himself or herself, so involved can judge the richness of growth from a particular experience. Per-haps, too, that judgement can only be meaningfully made through a time perspective allowed only well after the experience.

Breadth of exposure to life and even exposure to events high in growth potential is impactful only if one is open to such. Lack of personal openness limits the effects. For exposure to be real experience, there must be an openness to taking it in, and without that there can be no personal growth or transformation. Such openness implies presence, or to use the Buddhist term, mindfulness. Being mindful, being aware, is an opening to the world and events to which one is exposed.

Awareness can be diminished by the several organismic choices we refer to variously as defense mechanisms of the ego in the psychodynamic theories or contact boundary disturbances in Gestalt therapy theory. By means of these we may limit our openness to experience, shutting out and distorting that which our egos deem too threatening. Thus we may dull our awareness by deflecting that which seems too intense to receive more directly or by desensitizing our perceptive systems. And, too, we may confuse our awareness through introjections, projections, and confluence when the responsibility of our being a genuine and authentic person feels too great an existential risk. The list of such awareness clouding maneuvers is long and the dynamics of these maneuvers varied enough to invite considerable study. Used individually or in synergistic combinations, their efficiency in denying and distorting reality bespeaks their effectiveness in creating mindlessness or clouded awareness and, in turn, a diminished impact from one's exposure to the world.

It should be clear, then, that breadth of experience has meaning for growth in personhood only insofar as that experience is not denied depth. If kept superficial through the insulating effect of clouded awareness, experience is superficial and of little impact on the person. Awareness, then, is the nexus between breadth of experience and depth of experience. Or, to be more precise, one could say that it is a certain critical level of awareness that allows mere exposure to become growthful experience.

Often, as in the case of a job application or interview, experience is evaluated only in terms of the number of times interviewees have been exposed to some situation or the length of time spent exposed to the situation. Questions such as "How many times have you done that?" or "How many years of experience do you have doing that?" are inadequate to the extent that they fail to take into consideration the depth of the experience.

But, just as some attend primarily or exclusively to the dimension of breadth in considering experience, others may attend to depth to a more or less exclusion of breadth. Take, for example the view expressed by Kafka (quoted in Schoen, 1994, p. 82).

> You do not need to leave the room. Remain sitting at your table and listen. Do not even listen, simply wait. Do not even wait, be quite still and solitary. The world will freely offer itself to you to be unmasked, it has no choice, it will roll in ecstasy at your feet.

Clearly, awareness is a necessary condition for meaningful and growthful experience. Without awareness there is only exposure. So important is awareness that in Kafka's view, richness can emerge even from exposure to the simple and prosaic. He came close to implying that awareness is all that is necessary, that awareness is both necessary and sufficient for deep experience.

If great depth of experience can follow from awareness of relatively ordinary exposure, consider, then, what can emerge when such mindfulness is brought to bear on a rich sampling of the world and life events. Together, such breadth and depth result surely in a life abundantly lived. And such a life surely results in enhanced personhood.

Living life abundantly requires a certain courage and boldness. Not only does it mean to eschew the use of the awareness clouding defense mechanisms, but it means to try out life, to experiment. It means to take reasonable risks and allow for the expansiveness which is part of the natural rhythm of contact with the world and withdrawal into self (Smith, 1985).

Richness and fullness of personhood is, then, a reflection of breadth and depth of experience. This personhood represents a certain consciousness, and as Ram Dass (1973, p. 28) has suggested, " . . . therapy is as high as the therapist is." If, as he suggested, one's patients will only be as free as one is himself or herself, then one would do well to work on oneself. To quote Ram Dass (1973, p. 6) once more, " . . . the only thing you have to offer another human being, ever, is your own state of being . . . you are only doing your own being, you're only manifesting how evolved a consciousness you are. . . . That's the only dance there is!"

And that is the dance of *the person of the therapist.*

REFERENCES

Adam, M. (1976). *Wandering in Eden.* New York: Alfred A. Knopf.

Bugenthal, J. (1971). The humanistic ethic–The individual in psychotherapy as a societal change agent. *Journal of Humanistic Psychology, XI,* 1, 11-25.

Lambert, M., & Bergin, A. (1994). The effectiveness of psychotherapy. In A. Bergin & S. Garfield (Eds.), *Handbook of psychotherapy and behavior change.* (Pp. 143-189). New York: Wiley.

Ram Dass. (1973). *The only dance there is.* Garden City, NY: Anchor/Doubleday.

Schoen, S. (1994). *Presence of mind.* Highlands, NY: The Gestalt Journal Press.

Shepherd, I. (1992). Teaching therapy through the lives of the masters: A personal statement. In E. Smith (Ed.), *Gestalt voices* (pp. 239-240). Norwood, NJ: Ablex.

Smith, E. (1985). *The body in psychotherapy.* Jefferson, NC: McFarland.

On Satir's Use of Self

Au-Deane S. Cowley
Ramona S. Adams

SUMMARY. One of Virginia Satir's greatest gifts to the world was the use of herself as an instrument of healing. By daring to use all of her-self–body, mind and spirit–the connections Virginia made with others were warm and real. Besides being authentically caring, Satir worked out of a pluralistic and comprehensive theoretical base to individualize each intervention. By co-creating strong, trusting relationships she in-spirited others with her own life-force energy, and enabled them to become more fully human. Able to put her own ego needs aside, Virginia modeled how to join common sense with a sense of high purpose. *[Article copies available for a fee from The Haworth Document Delivery Service: 1-800-342-9678. E-mail address: <getinfo@haworthpressinc.com> Website: <http://www.HaworthPress.com>]*

KEYWORDS. Self esteem, trust, healing, life-force energy, uncondi-tional affirmation, spirituality, empowerment, multicultural, integrative, pluralistic, wholeness, self-transcendence

One of Virginia Satir's greatest gifts to the world was the use of herself as an instrument of healing. She did not hold back or save

---

Au-Deane S. Cowley, PhD, is Corresponding Author, Professor Emerita of Social Work, University of Utah, 1931 South Moor Drive, Salt Lake City, UT 84117.

Ramona S. Adams, PhD, is Professor Emerita from the Graduate School of Social Work, University of Utah.

Address correspondence to: Au-Deane S. Cowley, PhD, 1931 East South Moor Drive, Salt Lake City, UT 84117.

[Haworth co-indexing entry note]: "On Satir's Use of Self." Cowley, Au-Deane S., and Ramona S. Adams. Co-published simultaneously in *Journal of Couples Therapy* (The Haworth Press, Inc.) Vol. 9, No. 3/4, 2000, pp. 51-68; and: *The Personhood of the Therapist* (ed: Barbara Jo Brothers) The Haworth Press, Inc., 2000, pp. 51-68. Single or multiple copies of this article are available for a fee from The Haworth Document Delivery Service [1-800-342-9678, 9:00 a.m. - 5:00 p.m. (EST). E-mail address: getinfo@ haworthpressinc. com].

anything. She used it all. Totally real and un-self-conscious Virginia taught by example that nothing can impact the human soul like another human soul. She understood, both cognitively and intuitively, that the process of healing is an interactive process that depends for its effectiveness much less on what one does than on what one is; much less on what one knows than on what one is able to help another human being to experience.

EXPERIENCING VIRGINIA

When Virginia walked into a room she filled it with the energy of her own fully human Self. At a level somewhere beyond all reason one could feel her power and sense her presence. There was a vitality and optimistic charge about her. Juices began to flow, and there developed an almost immediate physical and emotional connection between her and whoever else was present. An inexplicable sense of safety and security made the context feel like one big "holding environment" whether the site was an intimate room, a vast auditorium, or the whole outdoors.

Trying to dissect such an ineffable experience is like chasing a rainbow, yet there are some concrete criteria that can be articulated to give a flavor of how Satir worked with others. She co-created the following kinds of experiences:

1. the experience of warmth and the feeling that someone really cares, that what happens to you matters to someone else.
2. the experience of having someone listen carefully, and to take seriously what you have to say.
3. the experience of being encouraged by an empathic other to identify and verbalize your deepest truths, and by so doing, to become more intimately acquainted with your real self.
4. the experience of being able to talk freely and honestly without fear of being judged negatively or rejected if your values differ from hers, or from the norms of society.
5. the experience of total acceptance that allows you to feel that your value as a person is not tied to meeting external expectations.
6. the experience of being able to rebel, or even express hostility without being shamed for doing so.

7. the experience of trusting and being trusted by another human being who believes you can make responsible decisions for yourself.
8. the experience of connecting spiritually with someone who encourages you to live from your own Inner Truth.
9. the experience of being affirmed and respected by one who honors your right to grow and change.
10. the experience of a consistent and stable relationship with Being who is a healthy and fully human.

The experience of being totally accepted within a loving context not only builds self-esteem, it also frees one to share at deeper levels than before. Virginia's caring presence encouraged and inspirited others in ways that enabled them to confront and express long denied or hidden vulnerabilities. One person described how it felt to her to experience Virginia by saying: "When Virginia was near she brought joy back into people's eyes. We laughed and cried together. She literally infused energy into our bodies We came to life again!" (Bitter, 1980).

USING ALL OF ONE'S SELF

One of the reasons Virginia had such an empowering effect on others is that she valued and brought ALL of herself into the healing process. She modeled for clients the importance of owning one's shadowy pieces, and was not into playing roles dictated by others or by societal pressures. Her famous "Parts Parties" demonstrated her belief that every part of a person has value and can be used positively or negatively depending on the circumstances and the choices that one makes.

Satir was never intimidated by anyone's idea of what was professional. She allowed herself to be totally present with others. She chose not to internalize taboos against tenderness or touch. Instead she made an intentional choice to bring her whole self into the relationship. Her encounters with others included her physical body, her emotions, her cognitive powers, her social and interpersonal skills, and perhaps most importantly her spiritual dimension or soul.

Physically Satir was not afraid to use therapeutic touch even before it was accepted and utilized in medical schools to train doctors and nurses. Her hands and body language demonstrated that she was physically present with you. *Emotionally* she was confident and secure enough in her own self-worth to be transparent. If she felt the tears, the tears would fall. If something touched her funny bone, she would laugh and bring humor to lighten the moment. If she got stuck, she didn't mind asking the client's permission to "go fishing."

Cognitively Virginia was a brilliant tactician. She knew instinctively how to weave a therapeutic tapestry out of the many threads from gestalt, communication theory, psychodrama, body work, hypnosis, use of right brained imagery, "visions," and visualizations, or anything else that she sensed might be helpful. By extending her work in the later years to include the *spiritual* dimension, Satir demonstrated her pluralistic and integrative understanding of what later became known as The Four Forces: First Force, psychodynamic theories; Second Force, behavioral and cognitive behavioral theories; Third Force, experiential, humanistic and existential theories; and Fourth Force, Transpersonal Theory (Cowley, 1993).

On the *social or cultural* level, Virginia understood the critical importance of making connections across territorial, ethnic or racial boundaries. Her love for humankind led her to seek out and interact with varying cultures and creeds across the globe. She was as much at home participating in a ritual dance as she was in a traditional academic classroom, and she was as completely comfortable in an Indian dwelling as she was in an Asian, Soviet, Polynesian or European setting.

THE THERAPIST AS A "REAL" PERSON

Being real and being human were concepts that Satir used synonymously. She believed that one's strengths as well as one's weaknesses both played a critical part in relationship, and that any honest encounter demanded wholeness. Consequently, Virginia claimed the right to be imperfect and still be helpful. Even though trust, authenticity, warmth, respect, and generativity were held up as therapeutic ideals, conscious effort was focused on legitimizing the idea that limitations are also an integral part of any real human being and/or the relationships people co-create together. Therefore, for Virginia, a whole relationship ought never be mistaken for a polite dance between placators.

> No human being is so perfect that he will never indulge or engage in behavior which appears to be either unloving or untrust-

ing. This is not possible for human beings, as you well know. What I am saying is that no human being can have his behavior reflect continual love and continual trust. It does not work that way. (Satir, Stachowisk, & Taschman, 1977, p. 47)

The realness essential to the therapeutic encounter, or any healthy relationship, is not a gift of the Gods, but a by-product of the conscious evolution of one's higher Self.

THE IMPORTANCE OF EARLY RELATIONSHIPS

Like the lasting impact of some first impressions nothing affects an individual's evolutionary potential more than his/her earliest experiences. Virginia was unrelentingly clear that we all get our most indelible attitudes and beliefs about self, others and the world from our earliest caretakers. Since no one has a perfect infancy or childhood, many individuals require corrective relationships with therapeutic others in later life in order to build ego structures that were neglected or wounded during early developmental stages. A constructive bonding with a consistent, loving and accepting other is a basic human need that must be met somewhere along the way if an individual is ever to achieve full potential.

Kaufman (1989) (as well as many others) has focused on how important the establishment of an early, interpersonal bridge is to healthy human growth and development. Ideally such a bridge is formed between parent and child out of shared experiences that build trust between them from birth. When there are failures or gross inconsistencies in the parent/child relationship, one or both may feel unappreciated or misunderstood. When a shaming response is evoked in significant relationships, a loss of self esteem and sense of connection results. This kind of experiential erasure, if repetitive, lies at the very core of many of the narcissistic wounds of childhood. Developmental deficits are often underneath the presenting problems adult clients bring into therapists' office. Many people are actually seeking relief from the unrelenting happiness anxiety and self-sabotage that flow out of a shame-based childhood.

Kaufman has pointed out how difficult it is for a therapist as surrogate parent, to heal or mend the fragile bridge to the heart once it has been ruptured. Other developmental theorists have also held that the role of therapist or healer is often similar to that of a nurturing parent. This is something Virginia knew even before literature about re-parenting was written. Early in her career Virginia was given the title of "mother," by Jay Haley. In 1962, as Haley sought to categorize therapists and theories of marriage and family counseling, he dubbed Satir's approach "The Great Mother School" because, according to him, she "emanates a benevolent capacity and attempts to generate a friendly atmosphere" (Haley, 1962, p. 94).

It was Virginia's warmth, her smile, her capacity to love, her wholehearted acceptance of others that made such a difference in the many lives that she touched. These qualities of spirit enabled her to build bridges between hearts and souls and to free blocked energy for personal growth.

BUILDING TRUST THROUGH CONFIRMATION

One of the uses of self necessary to the success of the therapeutic process is the capacity to provide an experience of genuine interpersonal confirmation. Only complete acceptance and validation from a trusted "other" can help a person overcome deep levels of early shaming and mistrust. When one has experienced conditional love or pseudo confirmation in childhood, it often requires that a person establish a false self or persona in order to survive or to please his/her caretakers. According to Friedman, what is needed most in therapy, later in life, is a confidante who has the capacity to honor and confirm the person's "dynamic existence-specific potentiality" (Friedman, 1988, p. 35), or real self. Like Friedman, Virginia believed that the establishment of a confirming dialogue with a sincerely caring person was the key that might unlock the prison of aloneness and free the frightened inner child from the isolation of feeling separated from self and others.

> If disconfirmation or the absence of confirmation lies at the root of much psychopathology, then confirmation lies at the core of healing through meeting. Healing through meeting is that therapy that goes beyond the repair work that helps a soul that is diffused and poor in structure to collect and order itself to the essential task–the regeneration of an atrophied personal center. (Friedman, 1988, p. 34)

It was in this kind of healing through meeting that Satir really excelled! She made a person feel ALL important and totally visible, confirmed, validated, valued, and loved. It was this style of Virginia's that worked magic in her personal and professional relationships. It engendered a complete sense of trust that provided a space into which one could grow.

Jean Houston described this ability to quicken another's growth as follows:

> The greatest of human potentials is the potential of each one of us to empower and acknowledge the other . . . The process of healing and growth is immensely quickened when the sun of another's belief is freely given. This gift can be as simple as "Hot dog! Thou art!" Or it can be as total as "I know you. You are God in hiding." Or it can be a look that goes straight to the soul and charges it with meaning. (Houston, 1982, p. 123)

Virginia's capacity to gift another with the look that made them feel totally "known" was often the main impression or felt sense that one remembered after an encounter with her.

TRUST ENABLES ONE TO RE-WRITE PERSONAL HISTORY

To consider the re-vision of one's view of self, others, and the world is very difficult. Clients, whatever their age, need to know that they have total acceptance from a trustworthy parent figure before they are willing to be open about their past or willing to risk consideration of new behaviors. This is especially true since the old brain is busily telling them that they may not survive if they dare to do anything to change the programs that were entered in their computer-like minds by their families of origin. Sometimes these programs become part of experience at a preverbal level. When one is attempting to make changes at the core level of being, one must believe that the extreme vulnerability and anxiety that change at that deep level creates will be honored and protected by a trustworthy person of integrity. In a very real way no one wants to take a risk unless it is safe.

> Without the existential trust of one whole person to another, there will be no realization on the part of the patient of the need to give up into the hands of the therapist what is repressed. Without such

trust, even masters of method cannot effect existential healing. (Friedman, 1988, p. 35)

To work at this level of authenticity and ego-integration requires that a therapist balance Erikson's (1950) key developmental crises while moving toward: a differentiated sense of self (identity), a capacity for closeness or intimacy, a generative ability to care, and enough wisdom to defeat despair. Being this kind of self-actualized person is a necessary prerequisite that enables one human being to reach out in healthy ways to another with the kind of fidelity and consistency on which trust is built in the healing context. According to Virginia:

> Trust is relatively easily engendered if you are congruent. It usually takes a minimum of three interchanges for a person to have trust in someone else. But however long it may take, the building of trust precedes everything else. (Satir et al., 1977, p. 134)

No one modeled more succinctly the art of developing trust than Satir. Having no hidden agendas and requiring no defense mechanisms to protect her ego, she was real because she felt no need to prove anything to anyone. Sometimes with no net at all Virginia helped others leap into the void they may have been avoiding. They knew she would take the leap with them. Her effectiveness in part was anchored in her capacity to commit so totally to the process. Virginia knew that it is always easier to tolerate the fear of exploring your own dark places if you are able to hold onto the hand of a trusted friend.

UNDERSTANDING THE PROCESS OF CHANGE

Satir gave considerable thought to the elements that constituted the process of change. Her firm belief in the sacredness of each human being resulted in her ability to teach people how to access a sense of their own divinity by listening to their own inner truth. As Virginia's clients began to sort things out and to grow, she encouraged them to take risks, to try new things, to reach out in different ways to test their own abilities, and above all, to trust their own judgment.

Satir did not impose her own values on others or ask people to turn out in prescribed or predetermined ways. Instead, she encouraged others to clarify, refine, and internalize their own values so they could ultimately leave the counseling relationship with a clear sense of who they were and what they believed. The ultimate goal was to help others to be able to operate successfully on their own as they sought their self-determined pathways.

In writing about the process of change Virginia saw *trust* as the critical first step (Satir et al., 1977). The second step was the development of *awareness* and for her, this always involved an experiential component. After awareness came a new level of *understanding* which meant that an expanded repertoire of options could now be opened up to include some new attitudes and behaviors. Only then could the person have a viable chance of getting out of repetitive ruts and old, destructive patterns and learn to tolerate the elements of novelty and surprise so essential to maintaining life-force energy. *Practice* was the next action called into play. Opportunities were created so individuals could integrate and perfect new ways of being in their lives and relationships. Each success added a new spiral of trust and self-efficacy. By achieving enriched levels of awareness new possibilities came into view. By integrating more competent behaviors changes occurred, and ultimately, a more empowered life was ready to be lived.

CHECKING HER PREMISES

Satir saw her work based as much in philosophy as in science. She had continually evolving premises about human nature and human growth. Four of her leading assumptions were:

1. Underlying every behavior is a reasonable or honorable motive. People are doing what they have learned to do and this is the best they can do in the circumstances.
2. Everyone is healable, and healing is inherent in the therapy process.
3. Mind and body are part of the same system. Physical vitality and emotional well-being are related. In therapy all avenues of access should be used. (Satir identified eight such avenues, including: physical, intellectual, emotional, sensual, interactional, contextual, nutritional, and spiritual.)
4. Self-esteem and effective communication beget one another. A person's self-esteem affects choice of spouse, the nature of the marital relationship, the needs expressed in the parent's rela-

tionship to their children, responses to stress, abilities to cope, flexibility, abilities to deal with differences and ambiguity, and enhanced freedom to grow and flourish. (Woods & Martin, 1984, p. 7)

In some of her last published words Satir expanded her earlier ideas about the process of change to put spirituality at the very core of the process:

I consider the first step in any change is to contact the spirit. Then together we can clear the way to release the energy for going toward health. This is spirituality in action. (Satir, 1988, p. 341)

By putting her spirit in action Virginia played various roles including: ally, devil's advocate, teacher, mother, antagonist, friend, or whatever–but always the role of a mature and trustworthy, fully human Being.

TEACHING AS AN INTEGRAL PART OF THE WORK

Satir often called her work "training for becoming more fully human," and she taught through demonstration, video, books, workshops, therapeutic modeling and her own life. She taught that the use of self was much less a result of mastering certain theories or techniques than a process of becoming a certain kind of person. Long before experiential therapies became popular, Virginia's work was replete with right hemisphere interactions. She believed this modality owed its effectiveness to the fact that it accessed pathways that differed from linear, left-brained, talk therapies. This difference in approach helped her interventions to avoid mental pathways that contained well-thought-out defenses and avoidance patterns.

Satir insisted that the exclusive use of talk therapy was not what changed lives. She believed that people changed only when the right hemisphere was also activated and they had some significant, emotional experiences that touched their lives at deep, affective levels. Synchronistically, the work of Gershen Kaufman (1989) has posited that the human's earliest, pre-verbal impressions are activated through affect, and imagery, and only through talking if language was present when they occurred. Thus, it would seem that Virginia's focus on experiential interventions has theoretical support.

Virginia wove all of her theoretical premises together, in each here and now moment, to create an integratively unique style all her own. With a firm conviction about the importance of individualizing the corrective experience she delighted in creating specific interventions for each client-system with which she worked. Through the use of her Self and her amazing capacity to reach out to others, Virginia created an atmosphere where people were enabled to experience life differently. In her presence many felt, perhaps for the first time, safe enough to put self-discovery ahead of self-defense.

Proponents of neuro-linguistics programming studied Virginia Satir and Milton Erickson to see if they could determine what it was about both of them that resulted in their having such an extraordinary capacity for building rapport with another. They concluded that whatever it was, it allowed them to become synchronized with another's internal processes in such a way that there was a kind of matching of the unconscious of one with that of the other that made the pull to connect almost irresistible (Woods, & Martin, 1984, p. 161). In her matter-of-fact way Virginia described this phenomenon as "finding another's rhythms and joining with them" (Simon, 1989. pp. 38-39). Interestingly enough, in ancient Greece they used the term "dromenon" to describe "a therapeutic rhythm, a dance of renewal that brings the participants into contact with a larger universe and a deeper understanding" (Houston, 1982, p. xxiv). One might wonder if "finding another's rhythms and joining with them," was Virginia's way of intuitively linking to the holonomic reality of the All.

BECOMING A CERTAIN KIND OF PERSON

Satir taught that becoming fully human was the supreme task of human growth and development. Like others who participated in the human potential movement after World War II, she was a believer in the ability of people to transform their lives to levels of exceptional well-being that far exceeded what most people considered as optimally healthy or normal (Walsh & Shapiro, 1963). She internalized Martin Buber's (1958) thesis that the healing which is also wholing "can only be attained through the person-to-person attitude" or an I-Thou relationship. Such a relationship is "founded on mutuality, trust, and partnership" (Buber, 1958, p. 132). It was also clear to Satir that to nurture a sense of wholeness in another the facilitator must first become a relatively "whole" person herself. Virginia was not content with aspiring to be merely "self-actualized," according to Maslow's earliest hierarchy of human needs (Maslow, 1968). She knew that the nurturing stance required of those in the helping professions demanded a capacity to focus on the other, and to put aside one's own ego (Walsh & Vaughn, 1980). Like Maslow in his later years, Satir also held that self-transcendence, not self-actualization, was the epitome of health and human potential (Maslow, 1971). Building on that bigger vision of the possible human, Ken Wilber has developed a model of the full spectrum of consciousness that includes the spiritual or transpersonal domain (Wilber, Engler, & Brown, 1986).

GOING BEYOND EGO

Taking the concept of self-transcendence to another level of specificity, a seminal author in transpersonal literature, Frances Vaughn, has delineated criteria that describe a self-transcendent or trans-personal level of consciousness. Her criteria include:

1. integrated, articulated wholeness in contrast to undifferentiated oneness;
2. consciously cognized intuition in contrast to trance or passive, unconscious perception;
3. faith and grace in contrast to infantile dependence;
4. insight in contrast to undifferentiated perception;
5. spontaneity in contrast to reactivity and impulsiveness;
6. altruism in contrast to narcissism; and
7. purity of heart in contrast to ignorance (Vaughn, 1987, p. 270).

To observe Virginia working with others was an opportunity to witness a Being working at a self-transcendent level. She was not interested in small stakes. Not unlike Jean Houston (1981), who pointed out that the Greek root meaning of therapy is "Therapea" or "doing the work of the Gods" (p. 43), Virginia entered therapy to play a part in an intensely heroic struggle. She took her work with others seriously, considering it a sacred task.

> You see, I think all therapy is a life-and-death effort, and many of us do not recognize that. We are playing for high stakes–for the recovery of another human being. (Satir et al., 1977, p. 49)

All life for Satir was equally precious and sacred. Her social consciousness and spirituality permeated all that she said and did, as a therapist or as a person, because the two were one.

CREATING A LOVING CONTEXT FOR HEALING

Related to the challenge of being a certain kind of person is the challenge of being a certain way with others. For Satir, everyone was connected to everyone else as in the pattern that connects (Bateson, 1972). If she were still practicing today, she would have a hard time compartmentalizing her total commitment to her clients to meet current definitions of what constitutes a "dual relationship." Virginia's love was healing precisely because she was a loving friend as well as an effective therapist. This may have been her most courageous and therapeutic stance. Scientific evidence gathered by Dr. Dean Ornish over the last 20 years has led him to conclude the following:

> I have no intention of diminishing the power of diet and exercise, or for that matter, of drugs and surgery. There is more scientific evidence now than ever before demonstrating how simple changes in diet and lifestyle may cause significantly improvements in health and well-being. As important as these are, I have found that perhaps the most powerful intervention–and the most meaningful for me and for most of the people with whom I work, including staff and patients–is the healing power of love and intimacy, and the emotional and spiritual transformation that often result from these. (Ornish, 1998, p. 2)

How typical for the modern, scientific mind to dismiss without consideration anything unavailable to the senses. However, the mind that goes beyond scientific materialism is slowly opening to include other ways of knowing. The findings of respected empirical studies of the spiritual dimension are accumulating. They demonstrate beyond a shadow of a doubt that "scientific" knowledge alone often falls far short in explaining extra-sensory realities that have real, measurable effects, and which many people have experienced in their lives.

According to Ken Wilber (1998), when all one has is the "flatland" of scientific monism (p. 140), the deeper, interior levels of human experience are lost. He proposes utilizing the Integral approach of "expistemological pluralism" that recognizes at least three valid ways of knowing: (1) The eye of the flesh (empirical knowledge); (2) The eye of the mind (rational knowledge); and, (3) The eye of contemplation (spiritual knowledge or gnosis) (Wilber, 1998, pp. 17-18).

Hailed as the Einstein of consciousness studies, Wilber has written extensively about the kind of "category error" that occurs when one confuses the role of monological science, dialogical philosophy, and translogical spirituality by trying to see with the eye of the flesh, or the eye of the mind, what can only be seen with the eye of contemplation, (Wilber, 1998, p. 21). He has this to say about the high costs of ignoring transrational ways of knowing.

> The entire interior dimensions–of morals, artistic expression, introspection, spirituality, contemplative awareness, meaning and value and intentionality–were dismissed by monological science because none of them could be registered by the eye of the flesh or empirical instruments. Art and morals and contemplation and spirit were all demolished by the scientific bull in the china shop of consciousness. And there was the disaster of modernity (Wilber, 1998, p. 56).

Intuitively, Satir was ahead of her time. She was able to heal the physical, psychological, and spiritual wounds that she encountered in practice because she was respectful, not only of objective knowledge, but also subjective and intersubjective ways of knowing. By so doing, she was able to demonstrate the invisible powers of love and intimacy to heal others.

ACTIVATING THE SPIRITUAL DIMENSION IN THERAPY

Helping others develop holistically often took Virginia into unchartered territories. Virginia was generally recognized as one of the innovators of the approach that first brought whole families into the therapist's office together. Being the pioneer/scout she was, she was not afraid to again be labeled "unorthodox" or "nontraditional" later in her life. She could not abdicate the challenge of incorporating spirituality as yet another potential vehicle for actualizing potential. Virginia unabashedly shared her belief that we are all spiritual beings in human form, and that we have a pipeline to universal intelligence and wisdom through our intuition (Satir, 1988, p. 338).

> My personal ideas and understanding of spirituality began with
> my own experiences as a child, growing up on a dairy farm in
> Wisconsin. Everywhere I saw growing things. Very early, I un-
> derstood that growth was life force revealing itself, a manifesta-
> tion of spirit. (Satir, 1988, p. 334)

Opening up to goodness and to a more abundant life was always an
essential part of Virginia's approach. As her own spiritual development unfolded, helping people to free up their stagnant spiritual ener-
gies became an important and exciting part of her work with the
spiritual dimension. She described this phenomenon as follows:

> It was as though I saw through to the inner core of each being,
> seeing the shining light of the spirit trapped in a thick, black
> cylinder of limitation and self-rejection. My effort was to enable
> the person to see what I saw; then, together, we could turn the
> dark cylinder into a large, lighted screen and build new possibili-
> ties. (Satir, 1988, pp. 39-341)

Satir was not afraid to talk openly about how she considered all
human beings to be "energy, congealed in space." Her spiritual focus
was on the leading edge and some mistook her commitment to divinity
within as a "flaky" stance that put her out on a limb–away from more
legitimized ways to practice. She understood that there will always be
those who would like to reduce spirituality to an irrelevant place in the
therapeutic endeavor, but nonetheless, she continued to be as adamant
in expressing her convictions about the importance of engaging the
spiritual dimension in clinical practice as she was about expressing her
commitment to world peace.

> Fifty years ago, no one except those connected with religion
> would have thought that spirituality was an appropriate subject for
> discussion in a nonreligious context. Some may still see spirituali-
> ty as naive or irrelevant to the business of living. I believe it is our
> connection to the universe and is basic to our existence and there-
> fore is essential to our therapeutic context. (Satir, 1988, p. 334)

Virginia was not a person to be caught up in her own importance.
She described herself as using "common sense." Those who have
evaluated her impact on others, however, have acknowledged that she

had a flair for "clear, nontechnical exposition and charismatic presentation that endeared her to tens of thousands in person, hundreds of thousands through her books and millions through the media (Gurman & Kniskern, 1981, p. 25).

CARRYING ON THE WORK

Satir left the challenge to those who followed to take the next step toward cooperatively building a new world community. She not only made the call for us to consider the whole planet as the client system, but also called on us to move beyond exclusive and competitive professional titles. She preferred a more inclusive nomenclature like "holistic practitioner" for all helping professionals regardless of discipline.

Satir's capacity to change lives and evoke growth in others had a magical quality about it. If you made the mistake of suggesting that to her, she swiftly reminded you that each of us have within ourselves the same capacity as she had to influence individual and collective lives for good. Accepting Virginia's premise that there are no duplicate human beings, brings us inevitably to the question that concerns us now as therapists. Not, "How did Virginia use herself in therapy," but "How can each one of us become whole enough, integrated enough, and congruent enough to use ourselves in a self-transcending way with others?"

It was never Virginia's way to promulgate specific techniques, but rather to teach would-be therapists to become aware of their own internal responses, and to use them to produce change in others (Brown & Christensen, 1986, p. 16). A typically untechnical statement of Satir's about what constitutes "failure" in therapy will illustrate this:

> One of the things I discovered as I traveled all over the country is that the chief reason any family therapeutic endeavor fails is that the therapist does not know how to have the kind of communication that makes it possible for people to get "connected with their guts." This has nothing to do with intelligence, race, color, or anything else except the ability to put people in touch with themselves at the gut level. (Satir et al., 1977, pp. 37-38)

How each therapist accomplishes that affective task is a challenge that must ultimately be met differentially.

WALKING THE WALK

For all the lives she touched Virginia spent much of her own life away from her family and loved ones, traveling around the world alone. She recognized what prices she paid personally for making the choice to do so and was willing to pay it. She was willing to use her Self until she was all used up in her committed quest for a world of peace filled with people who were fully human. One of the finest statements about how others will or will not be able to copy or replicate Satir's use of self is found in a memorial piece written by Annie Garfield after Virginia's death:

> It is clear to me that some of us will carry on her work in our own ways. We will fall short and we will go beyond. We are simply OF her.

AUTHOR NOTE

Au-Deane S. Cowley and Ramona S. Adams are sisters. Professionally, both are social workers first, educators, administrators, and authors second. Each affiliated with the Graduate School of Social Work, University of Utah, and served as Associate Dean. Dr. Cowley was recognized by the University with a Distinguished Teaching Award. Dr. Adams served as Associate Dean of Students for the University, and was the recipient of the Perlman Award for counseling students. Besides teaching in the master of social work program, they taught various courses in the Honors Program and in the Community while each maintained a private clinical practice. Both are currently "retired."

REFERENCES

Bateson, F. (1972). *Steps to an ecology of mind*. New York: Ballantine Books.

Bitter, J. (1980). Virginia Satir: The experience of her impact on human relations. *Program of the 27th Conference of the Association for Humanistic Psychology*. Palo Alto, CA: Stanford University Press.

Brown, J., & Christensen, D. (1986). *Family therapy: Theory and practice*. Monterey, CA: Brooks Cole.

Buber, M. (1958). *I and thou*. New York: Scribner.

Cowley, A. (1993). Transpersonal social work: A theory for the 1990s. *Social Work, 38*(5), 527-534).

Erikson, E. (1950). *Childhood and society*. New York: Brunner/Mazel.

Friedman, M. (1988). The healing dialogue in psychotherapy. *Journal of Humanistic Psychology, 28*(4), 19-41.

Gurman, A., & Kniskern, D. (Eds.) (1981). *Handbook of family therapy*. New York: Brunner Mazel.

Haley, J. (1962). Whittier family therapy? *Family Process, 1*, 69-100.

Houston, J. (1981/winter). On therapeia: Jane Prettyman talks with Jean Houston. *Dromenon, III*(3), 37-43.

Houston, J. (1982). *The possible human*. Los Angeles: J.P. Tarcher.

Kaufman, G. (1989). *The psychology of shame: Theory and treatment of shame-based syndromes*. New York: Springer.

Maslow, A. (1968). *Toward a psychology of being*. New York: Van Nostrand Reinhold.

Maslow, A. (1971). *The further reaches of human nature*. New York: Viking/Compass.

Ornish, D. (1998). *Love & survival: The scientific basis for the healing power of intimacy*. New York: Harper Collins.

Satir, V. (1988). *The new people making*. Palo Alto, CA: Science and Behavior Books.

Satir, V., Stachowiak, J., & Taschman, H. (1977). *Helping families to change*. Jason Aronson.

Simon, R. (1980, January/February). Reaching out to life. *Family Therapy Networker, 37-3*.

Vaughn, F. (1987). A question of balance: Health and pathology in new religious movements. In Anthony et al., *Spiritual choices: The problem of recognizing authentic paths to inner transformation*. New York: Paragon House.

Walsh, R., & Shapiro, D. (Eds.) (1983). *Beyond health and normality: Explorations of exceptional psychological well-being*. New York: Van Nostrand Reinhold.

Walsh, R., & Vaughn, F. (Eds.) (1980). *Beyond ego: Transpersonal dimension in psychology*. Los Angeles: J.P. Tarcher.

Wilber, K., Engler, J., & Brown, D. (1986). *Transformations of consciousness*. Boston: Shambala.

Wilber, K. (1998). *The marriage between sense and soul: Integrating science and religion*. New York: Random House.

Woods, M., & Martin, D. (1984). The work of Virginia Satir: Understanding her theory and technique. *American Journal of Family Therapy, 12*(4), 3-11.

The Therapist's Many Faces

C. Jesse Carlock

SUMMARY. Focusing on Virginia Satir's Parts Party method, the author discusses its potential uses in helping therapists to expand self-concept and develop their personal resources. Both of these goals inevitably enrich the therapy process and increase therapists' versatility. The various phases in conducting a Parts Party are described with enough detail to give the reader a sense of the process and its potential benefits. A number of variations of the Parts Party are also included to stimulate the reader's creativity and to encourage the development of spin-offs. *[Article copies available for a fee from The Haworth Document Delivery Service: 1-800-342-9678. E-mail address: <getinfo@haworthpressinc.com> Website: <http://www.HaworthPress.com>]*

KEYWORDS. Satir, Parts Party, use of self, polarities, self, self-awareness, self-concept

Some 25 years ago, newly out of graduate school, I wrote a journal article promoting therapists' use of self in the therapeutic process. The paper was sent to reviewers. When I finally received feedback, I was horrified. The reviewers reacted negatively and vehemently to my ideas. The moral hairs on the back of their necks were definitely raised. They equated the theme, the therapists' use of self in the

C. Jesse Carlock, PhD, is a Psychologist in Private Practice for over 22 years, is a Clinical Professor with the Wright State School of Professional Psychology in Dayton, OH. Dr. Carlock is also a senior training coordinator for The Gestalt Institute of Central Ohio. She is the author of numerous articles and chapters and has recently published the 3rd edition of her popular book, *Enhancing Self-Esteem*.

[Haworth co-indexing entry note]: "The Therapist's Many Faces." Carlock, C. Jesse. Co-published simultaneously in *Journal of Couples Therapy* (The Haworth Press, Inc.) Vol. 9, No. 3/4, 2000, pp. 69-83; and: *The Personhood of the Therapist* (ed: Barbara Jo Brothers) The Haworth Press, Inc., 2000, pp. 69-83. Single or multiple copies of this article are available for a fee from The Haworth Document Delivery Service [1-800-342-9678, 9:00 a.m. - 5:00 p.m. (EST). E-mail address: getinfo@haworthpressinc.com].

therapeutic exchange, with misuse of the therapy relationship to satisfy the therapist's own feelings and needs. "Unethical!" they scolded. Naively, I had never expected such a backlash. Deciding to keep my ideas private for the time being, I relegated my paper to some dead file and never discussed it or the reviewers' reactions until several years later after entering Gestalt training. In that training and through my work with Virginia Satir, I found a home for my values and beliefs, which have been nurtured, expanded and clarified over many years.

Lopping off large chunks of ourselves in order to be "good therapists" is an enigma to me. To summarily cut off my feelings or any significant part of myself in the therapy exchange would render me hollow and deadened. But the conventional "rules" around being a "good therapist" and being "adult" are often so rigid and dichotomous they can choke the life out of the therapy. Such unquestioned and rigid rules can severely constrict therapists' expressive abilities, expansion of self, and authenticity critical to deepening the dialogue. Of course, clients differ in their readiness to use the presence of the therapist and enter into a more profound dialogue. Therapists must know themselves well and use sound clinical judgement in decisions about which expressions of self at any specific point in time are likely to further the dialogue and open the way to the next step in awareness. Therapists with enough maturity, can use the self as a powerful instrument of change through which healing can occur.

The more differentiated my awareness of myself, the greater ability I have to make choices about what to bracket and what to suspend in the interest of the client. Likewise, the broader my experiences, the more open I am to stretch myself beyond my habitual boundaries (without violating basic, strongly held, assimilated values and beliefs), the greater the number of potential resources I have to bring to the exchange, the wider range of clients I can effectively reach and the deeper we can go. Being open to a wide range of experiences allows for the high quality contact crucial to identifying with clients who bring a myriad of experiences to the therapy relationship. Knowing and accepting all parts of myself gives me greater choice over when to bring particular parts into play in a given circumstance, thereby improving my effectiveness. However, as Hycner and Jacobs (1995) point out, use of self in the therapeutic relationship requires the most skill, the most self-awareness, and the soundest of judgement since the potential for harm is as great as the potential for healing.

Satir's Parts Party method is a vehicle, which can be used to help therapists in several ways:

1. To assist the therapist in self-differentiation
2. To explore the impact of various parts of self on clients
3. To help therapists recognize how they can access various internal resources to help clients achieve greater gains
4. To resolve impasses in the client-therapist relationship
5. To improve therapists' overall ability to use the self in the therapeutic context
6. To foster the ability of therapists to meet clients with genuineness and openness

THE SELF OF THE THERAPIST

In March 1999, I attended a weeklong seminar, A Fresh Look at Gestalt Therapy, conducted by Erving and Miriam Polster, two internationally respected Gestalt therapists whom I highly admire. During this seminar Erving Polster lectured on some of his ideas regarding the formation of self and his view that the individual is host to a diversity of selves, concepts which are described more fully in his book, *A Population of Selves* (Polster, 1995). As I listened I was surprised to find that his ideas were strikingly familiar. Many of Erving Polster's ideas I had first written about in an unpublished paper, The Parts Party For Self-Concept Differentiation and Integration (1988) in which I describe a complex vehicle called the Parts Party, which Virginia Satir invented (see Satir, 1978; Carlock, 1988; Carlock (Ed.), 1999). I was first exposed to her Parts Party method at her month-long residential process community in Park City, Utah in 1981. Erving Polster's and Virginia Satir's basic ideas are quite similar.

Such a convergence of ideas among master therapists across theoretical lines is common. In the case of Erving Polster, an internationally recognized Gestalt therapist and Virginia Satir, an internationally recognized family therapist whose early training was rooted in Gestalt, this intersection of their ideas is not surprising. Yet each has a unique style and process of identifying parts and working with parts of self. However, both of these master therapists seek to help clients to become enough aware of their parts to empower them to make conscious decisions about when and how to bring parts into action to maximize personal efficacy. With regard to the self, both focus interventions towards helping clients develop a powerful, accurate, and multifaceted self. These same concepts, which they have applied to clients, can also be applied to therapists.

By helping therapists to develop an expanded, aware sense of self, their potency in the therapeutic milieu (as well as in all aspects of their lives) may be enhanced. This expanded awareness and development of self can be instrumental in:

- increasing effectiveness with a wider range of clients
- expanding repertoire of skills in intervening
- increasing awareness of parts of self which may contribute to therapeutic impasses
- increasing awareness of parts involved in counter-transference
- increasing ability to choose which parts to bring into play
- expanding awareness of how parts can join together to further goals
- strengthening ability to take charge of parts in service of higher functioning

I know of no better vehicle than Virginia Satir's Parts Party method (Carlock, 1988; Carlock (Ed.), 1999) to illustrate the make-up and internal dynamics of the self. In order to bring life to the internal processes, which Virginia Satir always believed enhanced the learning process; she transformed the parts into flesh and blood characters. Through this method, all the senses are involved and excitement builds as the characters (parts of the self) come to life. Various characters portraying the different parts of self are invited to a party. What unfolds in the course of the party is processed with the STAR (person for whom the Parts Party is given) to determine in what ways the external manifestations and dynamics at the party reflect what goes on internally. The Parts Party, a relatively untapped method, may be used in a variety of ways. In this paper, I will review various applications for helping therapists to increase their consciousness regarding the use of self in the therapy context.

VIRGINIA SATIR'S PARTS PARTY

It is beyond the scope of this paper to describe the Satir's original Parts Party method in sufficient detail for the reader to actually conduct a Parts Party. For a more complete description of the Parts Party method see Carlock (1988). Hopefully, however, enough detail will be provided to give the reader a sense of the process and its potential uses. The traditional Parts Party method requires three to five hours over the course of two sessions to thoroughly complete all of the steps which include a preparatory phase, initial interview, early phase, middle phase and late phase. The method requires a group large enough to allow for one role player for each of the self-parts identified by the person for whom the Parts Party is being given. A few extra people allow for additional parts to be added. Additional members of the group can also serve as process observers/scribes to record significant dynamics throughout the proceedings. What follows is a brief explanation of each phase of a Parts Party:

- The *preparatory phase* includes selection of the STAR (the person who volunteers to explore his/her parts) identification of self-parts, recruitment of role-players, selection of the setting, orientation of the STAR, and gathering of costumes and props.

There are a number of different ways to identify parts to be invited to the party. For example, in working with a therapist as the STAR, the therapist might be asked to pick an animal which best represents his/her personal style in therapy. The animal whose traits the therapist STAR describes is then explored as a projective. The polarity of each trait assigned to that animal may also be explored as potential disowned, hidden or undeveloped parts. This same method might be applied more specifically to explore stylistic ways the therapist behaves with a particular client (e.g., a client with whom the therapist feels at an impasse). Parts might also be defined in a more left-brain way. For example, the therapist might be asked what characteristics (s)he believes go into making a good therapist and what traits (s)he would use to describe him/herself.

Once the parts are selected, the DIRECTOR (conductor of the party) reviews the list of parts to examine how each part could be useful and how each part might get in the way. In the therapy context, the DIRECTOR would also note what patterns stand out and/or what parts seem to be missing, underdeveloped, or overdeveloped. For example, the DIRECTOR might notice that agentic qualities such aggressiveness, toughness and reserve of feelings may be overdeveloped while polar traits of receptivity, gentleness, and emotionality are missing or underdeveloped. As these parts are explored, the DIREC-TOR might work with the STAR to identify and revise beliefs associ-ated with such polar parts. At any time during the process, the DIREC-TOR may experiment with adding parts to bring better balance to the system, to achieve a specific goal, or improve functioning (e.g., add-ing a sense of humor, creativity, wisdom, persistence, spirituality, anger, sensuality). The STAR would be asked to note what impact these additions have on his/her internal system or on the STAR's interaction with others (e.g., collegial, supervisory relationship, client-therapist relationship).

Once the parts have been identified, the DIRECTOR may ask the STAR to assign a famous figure, fictional or non-fictional to each part. Famous people are selected to personify each trait or cluster of traits identified. For example, a part, which asks questions and tries to get to the bottom of things, might be assigned the role of *Detective Columbo*. A reverse process may also be used wherein the therapist STAR would be asked to identify famous figures whom they admire or intensely dislike. The therapist STAR would then describe what traits in each person stimulate his or her reactions. These characters, representing owned and disowned parts, would then become guests at the party. Many people have a fragmented self with separate, mutually alienated parts. By opening communication with these parts as well as other parts, whether they are viewed by the STAR as being assets or liabili-ties, integration may be furthered.

One goal of the Parts Party is to move the STAR towards greater wholeness, embracing owned, disowned, and hidden parts. This meth-od involves imaginatively dramatizing these hidden, partially owned, and covert parts in interaction with owned parts so as to re-associate alienated parts and deepen the STAR's assimilation of accepted and valued parts. This follows Beisser's (1971) belief that evolving the self requires a person to reclaim dissociated parts. Satir (1981) stressed that all parts are capable of being both positive and negative given the particular context and circumstance. She would agree that some parts might need to be toned down or modified by joining with other parts in order to be more useful.

- During the *initial interview* goals for the Parts Party are agreed upon. In the case of work with a therapist, some questions which might be appropriate are:

1. What would you like to have happen as a result of this experience?
2. With what kinds of clients do you have difficulty (stuck, bored, angry, impatient)?
3. What type of personalities do you enjoy or dislike in clients?
4. In your role as therapist what parts of yourself do you deliberately avoid showing?
5. What rules regarding bringing yourself into the therapy process have you learned over the course of your therapy training and experience?
6. How would you describe your therapy style?
7. In what ways would you like to be different as a therapist?
8. Which parts of you present problems for particular types of clients?
9. Which parts of you seem appealing to clients?
10. Which parts of you do you wish would come out more in your therapy with others?

- In the *early phase* of the party, several objectives must be met. An overriding goal is to establish trust and a good working relationship with the STAR. In addition to this, first on the agenda is a brief introduction to the Parts Party method describing the process and some of its purposes. Following the introduction to the method several processes follow:

1. Ice breaker: A short exercise to introduce participants to each other in order to give the STAR a brief impression of each participant follows. The exercise provides limited data for the selection of role players.
2. Selection process: The STAR chooses role players to act out each part. The STAR is asked to choose the first person that comes to mind to play each part. This redirects the person away from using logic and linear thinking and towards using sensing and feeling in making these choices. Those chosen must give a clear "yes" or "no" to the request in order to play a role. After role players are selected, the first session ends. In the interim, role players set about putting together costumes and props in order to convey the essence of the part.
3. Enrolling: In the second session, the leader directs the entire group, and most especially the STAR in a centering and ground-

ing experience. Then, with the role players now in their costumes and with their props, the STAR is asked to give a gesture, facial expression, physical posture, and a characteristic line of script to each role player. For example, if the therapist STAR identifies a part, *Detective Columbo*, this part might dress in an old wrinkled, frayed raincoat and worn shoes, wear his hair mussed as he scratches his head from time to time, and carry a small notebook and pen. In a low-key way he might also go around from guest to guest asking poignant questions and scribbling notes as they reply.

- The *middle phase* of the party is a stage of awareness building. The STAR, along with the DIRECTOR, observes from the sidelines (they are not actually guests at the party but are able to step into the party and step back and get an overview). As the party unfolds, the DIRECTOR and STAR may note such aspects as:

1. Power structures: Which part(s) emerge(s) as most influential in a positive or negative way?
2. Alliances, clusters: Who supports whom? Which parts seem to pair up or form groupings? Who shows an interest in whom? On what basis do they align?
3. What transformations have developed (often when parts engage with other parts changes begin to occur)?
4. Conflicts and splits: Between which parts are there disagreements or arguments? Who avoids whom? How and when do parts separate?
5. Cohesion: Is (are) there a part(s) which bring the guests together? Does a theme emerge? Is there a sense of unity? If so, along what lines does there seem to be unity?
6. Isolates: Who is on the fringes of the party? Who has difficulty relating to the other guests? Is this person ostracized or welcomed? By whom?
7. Tone and style of the party: How would you characterize the party (e.g., frenzied, relaxed, highly verbal, intellectual, emotional, no touching, lots of touching, little or lots of movement, loud or soft in tone, colorful, boring, exciting, loving, hateful, distant, close)? Use your own words. Metaphors may help.

8. What is missing and could be added to the party for balance, to perk it up, to calm the party, or to change it to a way that would be more satisfying?
9. Which parts are most attractive to the STAR? Most offensive?
10. Which parts could the STAR add that might help incorporate other seemingly less attractive or more frightening parts? For example a person might first want to add self-control before accepting sexuality.
11. What other patterns are apparent? For example, "I notice it is hard for the people at this party to see others feeling badly. Someone always rescues."
12. Do any of the guests remind you of someone around you when you were growing up? Who?

The types of interventions the DIRECTOR can make during the middle and late phases of the party are limited only by the DIRECTOR'S creativity. During the middle phase, in order to add emphasis, for example, one part might be asked to exaggerate itself while other parts are directed to stand in silence. In order to help the STAR own a particular part, (s)he might be asked to step in and play a part, which is underdeveloped in his/her personality. In order to enhance awareness, a group member might be selected to serve as an alter ego for the STAR and report what (s)he sees, hears, feels, and thinks throughout the process. Or, the DIRECTOR might ask one or more parts to speed up, repeat rapidly some action, sentence, gesture or sound. The STAR is also permitted to eavesdrop on conversations of a particular grouping while the other guests remain silent. After observing the group of parts, the DIRECTOR or STAR may choose to form a sculpture (visual picture) of the dynamics. By posing the players, molding their body postures and facial expressions, and adding gestures and movements, primary emotional stances and relational patterns may be conveyed. Parts may also be sculpted with a particular question in mind (e.g., "Show me how the system of parts reacts when you are confronted about some problem with your behavior or attitude" or "Now show me how you would like to react").

At various points during the party, the DIRECTOR calls "freeze" and moves with the STAR to interview particular guests to find out what they are experiencing and needing. Depending on what the guests are experiencing or needing, the DIRECTOR might ask guests to shift their posture, expression, sentence, or activity to better fit this. Guests might also be asked what action they could take or what other guests might be enlisted to help satisfy the need or manage the feeling. Usually, transformations begin to occur at this point.

At frequent intervals throughout the party, the DIRECTOR asks the STAR to reflect on how what is happening at the party might reflect what the STAR experiences in him/herself. Awareness of the STAR's internal dynamics is expanded through the middle phase. Eventually, in the late phase of the party, the STAR begins to discover ways to move through conflicts, impasses, tensions, and other perceived difficulties as well as how to employ self-parts in more proactive ways.

- In the *late phase* of the party, the DIRECTOR attempts to help the STAR bring further harmony, coordination, and balance to the self-system. Methods to further this goal might include accentuating parts which need further development (e.g., emphasizing an intuitive part in a therapist who might favor the rational or logical), or identifying ways to interrupt negative patterns among guests by asking each guest to identify at least one way each part could respond differently. Surprise guests might also be added to represent resources needing development (e.g., adding a challenging part or directness to a therapist who might be overly soft or obscure). Feeling reactions are processed along the way and beliefs interfering with self-stretching are examined and, when appropriate, revised.

To facilitate empowerment of the STAR, (s)he is encouraged to assume a "control tower" position to take charge of the parts directing guests to behave as (s)he wishes. For example, the STAR might join several parts (e.g., tough, direct, compassionate and experimental) and direct them to take the lead in a certain direction (e.g., to interrupt self-pity). A STAR might ask one part to fade into the background, accentuate a part, or ask two parts to join together in managing a third part. As usual, the STAR is asked to draw parallels between what happens at the party with what happens or could happen inside the self, in the STAR's behavior in the world, and in the case the therapist as STAR, specifically in the therapeutic environment.

In the final steps of the late phase, the DIRECTOR tries to bring some closure to the party, work further towards a path of resolution of identified problems, achieve greater acceptance of each part (even negatively valued parts), and further integrate learnings. Homework assignments also foster greater integration.

The DIRECTOR then de-roles each participant, putting aside the part each played and coming back into his/her own skin. Lastly, during the wrap-up, role-players and observers/scribes share additional observations of the party as well as how each personally related to dynamics of the STAR's party and to the part each played. The STAR, role-players and any process observers may also be asked to develop specific goals and an action plan for each goal to assist in transfer of learning.

FURTHER APPLICATIONS FOR THERAPISTS

The Parts Party as designed by Satir can be a springboard for creating a variety of adaptations. The Parts Party can easily be combined with other methodologies as well. The method can be geared to fit the DIRECTOR'S personal style and strengths, to suit the particular setting and people resources available, and to correspond with the goal. To stimulate the reader's creativity, this section includes a brief description of Satir's Couples Parts Party (see Winter and Parker, 1991 for a more complete description) as well as a variety of less complex adaptations.

The Couples Parts Party, is a vehicle for exploring the dynamics between two partners. In a similar way, a DIRECTOR could use this vehicle to examine the dynamics between the therapist and another colleague, a therapist and a supervisor, or a therapist and a particular client. In the case of a therapist and a client, the therapist STAR would identify six or more traits (positively or negatively valued), which tend to emerge between the therapist and this particular client. The therapist STAR would also identify six or more characteristics (positively and negatively valued), which the client tends to display with the therapist. The STAR then chooses players for each role and each player gathers costumes, props, and is enrolled as described in the traditional Parts Party. Instead of inviting all to a party, however, each set of parts is lined up randomly behind two screens, the therapist's parts behind one screen; the client's parts behind another screen. The screens should face each other and be spaced about twenty feet apart to allow enough space for the interaction of parts.

One at a time and in random order, a part from each side comes out from behind the screen hiding the therapist's parts and, in role, spontaneously meets and interacts with a part which comes out from behind the screen hiding the client's parts. In this way, the STAR can begin to see various strengths and problem areas in this two-person system. For example, parts in conflict, parts that work together well, parts that reach impasses, and parts that bring strength or tension to the relationship will be observed. The DIRECTOR may help the STAR become aware of what parts might be activated to reduce or manage conflict, move through impasses, or further strengthen the relationship. Parts may also be added or the STAR may become aware of ways to access particular parts (open, blind or hidden) of the client.

This adaptation of the Couples Parts Party might also be used to explore difficulties in a relationship between two colleagues. In order for the experience to be positive, however, a base level of trust and good will must be present. In this case, each colleague would be asked to choose parts for the other, identifying what parts of the other are appealing and what parts each perceives as difficult in the other. Each partner is asked whether (s)he accepts the parts assigned by the other. If, for example, the therapist STAR does not accept a part assigned by the client (for example, judgmental), then the client is asked to pick this part for him/herself. In essence, Satir would treat this part as a projection. However, once the colleague agreed to accept this part, Satir would then reframe the same part for the assignee in order to encourage acceptance. "Do you have a part that decides what things are good and what things are not good? We'll call this the "decider" part." A similar process as described previously would then ensue.

Another less complex variation of the Parts Party would involve selecting the therapist's parts and then sculpting (described previously) the therapist STAR's parts. For example, the DIRECTOR or the STAR might sculpt the STAR sitting on certain parts, some parts arm in arm, a part trying to wiggle in from the back, two parts elbowing each other, a part isolated from the cluster and scurrying towards the main group in now and then, one part covering another, and so on. The DIRECTOR, in processing the feelings, thoughts and needs of the parts in the sculpture, may uncover beliefs or feelings, which need revision or attention. For example, if several parts are holding an angry part down, the DIRECTOR might explore the STAR's beliefs associated with anger as well as identify what parts the client uses to suppress that anger. Feelings and needs of each part might then be identified and honored and steps towards appropriate satisfaction of the need outlined and practiced. Parts may also be sculpted with a general goal in mind. For example, the STAR might be asked to show a configuration of his/her parts with clients in general (a view of the therapist's basic style). Parts may also be sculpted with more specific goals as well. For example, the STAR might be asked to configure his/her parts when facing a client who is hostile.

Even following the traditional Parts Party process only through the preparatory phase may be enlightening. As the process proceeds, the DIRECTOR might ask the STAR to identify which key family rules/ values or rules inculcated during training or supervision are manifested in the parts chosen and not chosen. For example:

1. Always be serious (omission of humorous or playful part).
2. Don't express anger (omission of a part that stands up for self or sets boundaries).
3. Always stay seated in therapy and keep good eye contact (loss of flexibility and liveliness).

To exaggerate what the DIRECTOR feels is an overdeveloped part or to accentuate an underdeveloped part, the DIRECTOR might ask the STAR to invite friends to a costume party. For example, if the therapist STAR has an overdeveloped contained part, (s)he might come as Nancy Reagan. By staying in role throughout the party, the therapist STAR's awareness of the constriction of this role may be heightened. Or, to encourage stretching, the therapist STAR might be asked to play a character that represents more openness and flexibility.

In another variation, a therapist might be asked to identify several therapists whom (s)he admires and to define what characteristics of each these therapists stand out as admirable. The DIRECTOR might then attempt to help the therapist own each of these qualities as projections, explore blocks around ownership, and identify ways to stretch in these directions. Experiments may be designed to facilitate this stretching.

Depending on the readers' facility with groups, large or small, a variety of offshoots of the Parts Party may be designed depending upon the particular goal. Though somewhat limiting, this work may also be done with individuals. Puppets, imagery, masks or other creative alternatives may substitute for role-players.

CONCLUSION

The beauty of Satir's Parts Party is its use as a powerful model of the ever-changing self. The Parts Party provides an external form for displaying the internal structure and dynamics of self, including the self-parts. Through the "control tower" position, the STAR learns how to step out and observe the process of the self as a whole, then with new awareness the STAR can choose to re-form elements or expand or contract in particular ways to meet specific goals in varying contexts. By stepping into the role of particular guests, the STAR may also experience the process from these vantage points, thereby gaining multiple perspectives. The STAR's facility with moving in to experience and moving out to observe is also enhanced.

Through the Parts Party method, therapists' awareness of themselves may be increased so that they can more fully and effectively use their personal resources in the therapy. Countertransferential vulnerabilities may also be spotted and explored. The Parts Party can easily be used in training and supervision of therapists. The method is both playful yet powerful. It can be used to illustrate the functioning of the self, in general, or to explore the self of the therapist specifically to increase self-awareness, to expand the self, to identify and resolve internal conflicts, and to identify and resolve dysfunctional relational patterns.

By developing a curiosity about self and exploring the self more fully, blind spots may be uncovered, rejected parts may be transformed or reframed, unrealized resources may be brought to awareness, and internal conflicts, projections, and faulty beliefs may be identified and revised. Through the Parts Party and its variations, chances are increased that therapists' use of self will bring healing, not harm to the therapeutic encounter; a genuine meeting versus acting out. When therapists are aware, accepting, and in charge of "their many faces," or "cast of characters" as Satir would say (1978), they can then more effectively help clients to explore their unique configurations of self.

REFERENCES

Beisser, A. (1970). The paradoxical theory of change. In J. Fagan and I. Shepherd (Eds.). *Gestalt therapy now* (pp. 77-80). New York: Harper.

Carlock, C. Jesse. The parts party for self-concept differentiation and integration. Unpublished manuscript, Peoplemaking Midwest, Carlock and Associates, 1105 Watervliet Avenue, Dayton, Ohio, 45420.

Carlock, C. Jesse (Ed.). (1999). *Enhancing self-esteem* (3rd ed.). Muncie, Indiana: Accelerated Development.

Hycner, R. and Jacobs, L. (1995). *The healing relationship in Gestalt therapy: A dialogic/self-psychological approach.* Highland, New York: The Gestalt Journal Press.

Polster, E. (1995). *A population of selves.* San Francisco: Jossey-Bass.

Satir, V. (1978). *Your many faces.* Berkeley, CA: Celestial Arts.

Satir, V. (1981, August). *AVANTA process community.* Park City, Utah.

Winter, J.E. and Parker, L.R.E. (1991). Enhancing the marital relationship: Virginia Satir's parts party. In Brothers, B.J. (ed.), *Virginia Satir: Foundational Ideas* (pp. 59-82). New York: The Haworth Press, Inc.

The Protean Therapist:
Molding and Remolding Herself

Nancy Small

SUMMARY. The subject of the following article is the protean journey therapists make as they adapt to changing situations and challenges in their own lives and the ultimate impact it has on their clinical work with patients. I have used the example of my own life, in which certain critical events have transformed me from a person with a rather ordinary perspective to someone who has come to appreciate the fragile nature of life with its rich tapestry of complicated ties and patterns. I have tried to demonstrate that significant events in my life and my personal development over the past thirty years have furthered my appreciation and treatment of my patients. I have also come to recognize that my patients' particular journeys, on which I have accompanied them, have similarly contributed to and enriched my life in myriad ways. *[Article copies available for a fee from The Haworth Document Delivery Service: 1-800-342-9678. E-mail address: <getinfo@haworthpressinc.com> Website: <http://www.HaworthPress.com>]*

Nancy Small, PhD, is a Clinical Psychologist in private practice in Oreland, PA, specializing in marital and family therapy and women's issues. She is Board-Certified in Family Psychology. As Assistant Professor in the Department of Psychiatry, MCP/Hahnemann Medical College, Philadelphia, PA, she has taught for many years. A previous contributor to the *Journal of Couples Therapy*, she has published in a number of local newspapers and has a monthly column, *For Women Only*, in the *Delaware Valley Parent's Guide Magazine*. Dr. Small is also host of a Philadelphia-based radio show, *A Small World*, offering an informative blend of psychological issues and features on the arts as a means of furthering self-expression and healing in the community. In her spare time, she indulges in her artistic endeavors (i.e., painting furniture with whimsical themes), and her work has been shown in a number of galleries throughout the Philadelphia area.

[Haworth co-indexing entry note]: "The Protean Therapist: Molding and Remolding Herself." Small, Nancy. Co-published simultaneously in *Journal of Couples Therapy* (The Haworth Press, Inc.) Vol. 9, No. 3/4, 2000, pp. 85-95; and: *The Personhood of the Therapist* (ed: Barbara Jo Brothers) The Haworth Press, Inc., 2000, pp. 85-95. Single or multiple copies of this article are available for a fee from The Haworth Document Delivery Service [1-800-342-9678, 9:00 a.m. - 5:00 p.m. (EST). E-mail address: getinfo@haworthpressinc.com].

KEYWORDS. Selfhood, therapist, journey, protean

Like a mound of clay, the person/therapist I am today has been pummeled, shaped and molded by life's experiences. In particular, the metamorphosis from the fragile, young structure that once defined me to the solid, still evolving creation that I am today came about through a series of challenging events and tragedies. Like the Greek God, Proteus, who transformed himself in response to crises, I too have altered myself over the past 30 years. In the process, I'd like to think that I've gained ever-widening perspectives, more creative problem solving and a greater empathic capacity. While all too painfully aware of the fragile nature of human existence, my own life, in general, and my clinical practice, specifically, have been enhanced by unforeseen forces–catapulting me out of a complacent, passive stance into a more proactive, assertive posture. As a result, I'd like to think that I am more fully present with my patients to intensify and enlarge both our relational experiences. Over the years, I have found this to be an exhilarating, life-enhancing journey.

The therapist I am today is an experienced, middle-aged woman who has covered considerable ground–from a college student studying psychology to a divorcée who knows first hand the cycles of birth, death, marriage, parenting, separation, divorce, and aging. In the genograms I draw for my patients, I can readily identify the family scripts or relationship patterns over generations that compel most of us to seek out our particular marital partners and play out our familiar dances, even when they are so hurtful. I certainly know my own family script by now, the one that determined the course that my life would take, although I could never have predicted some of the more dramatic events that would cross my path.

After having escaped a very frustrating and unhappy marriage three years ago, I hardly recognize myself as the shy, young woman who walked down the aisle three decades ago. In that faded picture of the past, I appear as an insecure girl/woman, who followed the traditional path of most Jewish girls of that generation–the one exception being my determination to pursue a full-time, life-long career. My father, a brilliant, but absent-minded inventor (e.g., known to place an electric razor in the refrigerator) was supportive of my doctoral work in psychology, but other relatives chided me for not having married, labeling me a spinster at age 24.

Finally, as I was about to embark on my clinical internship, I married a "nice Jewish doctor"–fulfilling my mother's and grandmother's wish that I "find a man to take care of [me] forever." My husband (whose mother set up our first date) and I, both loyal children, thus entered into what was essentially an "arranged marriage." This dynamic is one that I frequently encounter among many of my patients, whereby their selection of mates is founded on some underlying loyalty issue.

I empathize with my patients when they describe their courtship in glowing terms; yet, even in those descriptions, there are clues that will almost reliably predict what issues might doom the relationship. I should have seen the clues, at least with respect to my own marriage, almost from the start. During our short-lived courtship, for example, my husband to-be arranged an ice skating date at an indoor skating rink. I felt magically safe and protected as he, a proficient skater, held my hand while we circled the rink. Suddenly, I fell, whereby my fiancé laughed and skated right over my limp body–only stopping to fetch me, several rounds later, after some stranger rescued me. This scene was to be an apt metaphor for our relationship over many years, whereby my husband was unavailable, both physically and emotionally, during times of need.

As I know from my work as a family therapist, the first task of any newly married couple is to separate emotionally from the families of origin. In all the years of my marriage, my husband would not and could not–such was the rigid control his parents held over him–accomplish this critical task. From the outset, it was clear that I was never to come first in my husband's life. For our engagement, I was presented with a huge diamond ring, contrary to my wish for a modest, more personalized ring. "How could I disappoint my parents (who owned a jewelry business)?" was my future husband's response to my muted reaction. Rather than further hurting his feelings, I gracefully accepted the ring.

My husband's primary alliance with his parents was still apparent a year later when, at my sister's wedding, he chose to sit with his family rather than with me at the bridal table. By then, it was abundantly clear that any complaints I registered would go unheard. And so, I initiated a pattern that was to characterize most of my marriage: swallowing my feelings of hurt and betrayal, but also building up an arsenal of anger and rage that would take its toll on myself and my family. (So many years of counseling patients to openly express their feelings, yet a seemingly impossible feat for me to master!)

Given the divergent realities that my husband and I seemed to experience in our relationship (e.g., "I don't know what you're talking about," or "I don't remember," he would claim), I began to question my stability. Was there something amiss with me–as in my childhood, when my reactions or feelings were labeled as my "being oversensitive?" I can still hear my mother's very audible sighs, signaling her dissatisfaction with my eating habits (I never ate enough) or my appearance. Then there was her intrusiveness and vigilant control over every area of my life, inhibiting any independence I might show. Any comment I made about her bothersome behavior was typically met with "But I'm entitled–I'm your mother," rendering me powerless. My quiet, workaholic father, with whom I experienced an unspoken closeness, had a particular way of negating my accomplishments: "You know you're not as bright as your sister is; you just persevere (I was the one with the As and a Phi Beta Kappa key). Despite my parents' loving ways, they both seemed incapable of mirroring my joyful moments.

My background, then, dictated the kind of woman, wife, and mother I would be: one who never felt empowered to assert herself or to trust her feelings, someone who was always anxious about receiving acceptance and approval. Years later, I was able to recognize that my relationship with my self-absorbed and narcissistic husband was also a replication of my relationship with a mother who was immature and not able to see past her own needs, someone driven by fear and anxiety.

I cannot say that I was completely emotionally available and devoted to my husband, either, through the early years of our marriage. Almost from the onset, I was sucked into the powerful vortex of family loyalties myself. Returning from our honeymoon, I was greeted by my younger sister, Linda, who broke the first of a series of tragic news to me: "Something terrible has happened; Marci [my favorite cousin, only 17 years old] is dead–killed in a car accident." Screaming, I tried in vain to drown out the dreadful reality imposed upon me. Life was not fair, its scales totally unbalanced, I thought. Here I was, entering into a promising, joyful stage of my life, and there was my cousin, following her mother, my aunt (who lost a protracted battle with cancer years before), in death.

Adding to the despair that day, my beloved grandmother visited the family–her stiff gait, frozen face, and tremors strikingly apparent, all signifying a more advanced stage in the Parkinson's disease with which she was afflicted. Soon, the most nurturing and adoring figure of my childhood, who fed me homemade chicken soup along with immeasurable love, was in a nursing home. The profound emotional connection we once had (I was her first grandchild) faltered just as her health did. It was to be several heartbreaking years later before she was to die. Little did we suspect that another granddaughter, full of life, would also precede her in death.

An avalanche of losses was to come in the next five years. Soon after landing my first clinical job, I found myself confronting another major crisis in my life. My father was diagnosed with amyotrophic lateral sclerosis, also known as ALS but more commonly referred to as Lou Gehrig's disease, named after the famous baseball player who succumbed to it in his prime. My father was only 55 years old, the same age I am today–a painful reminder of my own mortality, just as I am settling into the post-divorce stage of my protean reconstruction.

The shock waves of my father's impending death were felt in every corner of my family's life. As motor neurons that previously fired smoothly in my father's brain started their suicidal course, leading to muscle wasting, physical deterioration and finally paralysis, we resorted to typical family roles. My sister, wanting so much to please my dad (even marrying a man my father would come to cherish as a son), soon presented my father with the most beautiful gift, his first grandchild, Scott. I slipped into my overly responsible role, grilled my neurologist husband about the illness, tracked my father's emotional state closely and tried to offer comfort to my mother.

God, however, was to visit even more cruel trials upon my family–events that were to overpower my father's own monumental, arduous journey towards death. For, one evening, at the very moment that my mother proclaimed that "things can't get any worse," a tragic drama was already unfolding in the turbulent seas off the coast of Florida. Just that morning, with storm warnings posted, my brother-in-law, fanatically insisted that my sister, now six months pregnant with her second child, accompany him on a boat outing. The last glimpse of my sister as she set off from the dock into rough waters was that of a beautiful young woman, shivering, with a blanket tightly wrapped around her pregnant body.

The world as I knew it abruptly exploded early the following morning when my husband nudged me from a deep sleep to announce "some bad news." Fearing for my stricken grandmother or father, I never expected to hear what came next: "It's your sister. She's lost, lost at sea–they can't find her." I hardly recognized the animalistic shriek that came from a depth inside of me I had never even touched. I felt the sharp, unfathomable pain of a phantom knife ripping my heart to shreds.

I came to know grief on the most intimate level–not only for myself, but also for parents losing a cherished child. Rushing home that day, I hugged my grief-stricken mother, who tightly clung to me, as if to hold onto the other daughter, lost, as well. Meanwhile, my father, in his familiar barcalounger in the den, appeared as some petrified figure welded onto the arms of his chair. Rigidly resisting my embrace, he appeared too far-gone to ever be humanly comforted again. My father barely survived another five years only to die again at the hands of what I considered a merciless God.

My cherished sister, my only sibling, 20 months younger than me, abruptly and completely vanished from our lives. With the Coast Guard and the Navy engaged in an extensive search of the wind-battered area, the sea yielded up nothing. No boat, no body, not even a shred of clothing. Linda, only 27 years old, could only be presumed dead in the freezing, shark and barracuda infested waters. Her husband had been found the next morning on a sandbar five miles from where he alleged that the two had abandoned a disabled motorboat.

Immediately after my sister's death, my brother-in-law abruptly restricted my parents' visits to their only grandchild, 11 months old. In a bid to inherit her estate, he also pressed for a declaration of death, a mere two months after her disappearance. Suspicions arose, substantiated by the detectives and lawyers we hired and by a personal trip down to Florida that I made. However, we failed to uncover any physical evidence on which to build a legal case against my brother-in-law. In a final victory for our family, however, the estate went to Linda's son instead of her husband–to be held in a bank trust until my nephew turned 18 years of age.

A cut-off ensued. It was to be 18 years later that I conducted my long overdue search for my sister's son and found him attending a Southern college. My clinical experience, including my expert knowledge of family systems, certainly helped prepare me for this role of a lifetime. Without his father's knowledge (that was ultimately my nephew's decision), I reclaimed a nephew who had never even known I existed. Meanwhile, my mother had the long-awaited opportunity to reunite with her precious grandson. ("It's like a blind date," she announced when she met him in person, her adored baby grandson all grown up.)

Unfortunately, despite many celebratory get-togethers, including family vacations and my nephew's professed bliss at our reunion, he rarely calls now. The issue of divided loyalties (a problem commonly observed in my clinical practice) and the burden of secrecy related to his newfound family, must have tugged mightily at his heartstrings. I am comforted by the fact that he has, however, maintained contact with his beloved grandmother.

My sister's mysterious disappearance 28 years ago colored my whole life thereafter. It was as if my sister pulled me overboard with her, and barely able to breathe, I have been fighting the undertow that threatens to push me down into black nothingness. The nothingness is a big D–no, not death, but something just as compellingly brutal and frightening: Depression. For so many years, I swam to keep afloat in the murkiness of depression that pressed to cut off my very breath and existence. I came to know, all too well, what my patients' despair and depression felt like. I also experimented with the same pharmacological agents that were prescribed for my clinically depressed population. Since I was subject to so many of the medications' side effects, I could empathize with any discomfort my patients experienced as well.

A refuge after my sister's death and beyond has always been my total absorption in my patients' world, which has given me relief from my own tortured one. Here was a space where I could focus on others' concerns, where I learned to trust my instincts and realize a different, bolder persona than the one I assumed in my personal relationships. It was here that I gave birth to the self-confident woman I am today.

I also found relief in my own on-going therapy over many years. During the darkest days, I saw a psychiatrist, who drew out the fury that threatened to consume me. From that personal experience, I learned to not back off from my patients' rage, knowing that its expression would neither destroy them or me.

My husband, unconscious of his own rage towards his alcoholic, cold and controlling mother, fled from any feelings I expressed. As a defense, he developed denial to a high art form. His general indifference to my accomplishments or state of mind (e.g., when refusing to attend a party less than a week after my father's death, I was chastised: "I don't know why you're so upset–you knew he was going to die") only fueled my depression and feelings of isolation. The many marital therapies we entered into were unsuccessful. We certainly never experienced the renewal of loving, close feelings that I witnessed among the many couples I treated.

Additionally, my husband's subtle, passive-aggressive ways of undermining me, especially with our two children, were taking their toll. He modeled his ungiving ways to the children by refusing to give me birthday gifts because "birthdays weren't important" to him. He also formed an alliance with my daughter, comforting her in her bedroom after she would verbally assault me, deferring and catering to her at will–all contributing to what I perceived as an emotionally incestuous relationship. As a family therapist, I knew that this was totally dysfunctional, but I felt powerless in my attempts to break his hold over her. The many therapists we saw also failed to impact on this relationship. When my husband tried to vent his unspoken anger through our son, following my daughter's departure for college, I knew the situation would never change. Finally, faced with the horrifying fear that I might become as emotionally removed as my husband, my departure became imperative. I bolted.

Through the many years of my personal therapy, I have come to realize that my marriage had become an emotionally abusive relationship in which I was subtly denigrated, invalidated and stonewalled–that anytime I confronted my husband with the truth, some punishment would invariably follow. This has prompted me to be acutely sensitive to the ways in which women, in particular (although not exclusive to them), can be cruelly scarred by continuing verbal or emotional battering. In fact, this propelled me to write a series of articles on this phenomenon, which was widely received. I have subsequently run groups for this abused population, in which I focus on empowering women to find their own voices and to be fully themselves.

I now am in a happy place, and it embraces much more than a professional life and my wonderful children. It has expanded to include many creative outlets, which began several years before my marital separation and helped propel me into a new, more expansive space, especially within myself. I live in an old cottage surrounded by my grown children's art work, my painted furniture (which has launched a second part-time career), and piles of writings which have helped to define my once feeble voice. There are intimate, true friends in the picture. Then there is my bounteous flower garden, vigorously blossoming with color and form, which nourishes my protean spirit and soul.

Given the terrain I have traversed over the years, I continue to be impressed with the compelling power of transference whereby a number of my patients view me as a perfect human being–having a perfect life, perfect family, perfect career, with no blips in my personal happiness. One interesting case stands out, however, whereby my professional and personal lives intersected in a provocative manner. A complex and bright young female patient, who saw me as leading a flawless and successful existence (when I disappointed her in sessions, though, she was not averse to exploding in rage at me!), surreptitiously tried to obtain as much information about me as she could.

In her search, she came across one of my published articles, "The Other Part of Me" (Tessler, 1994, January/February), which recounted the profound impact my sister's loss had on me. Ironically, this woman had spent years in therapy with me trying to complete the mourning process with respect to her own younger sister, who had died many years earlier. In discovering that I myself had had a similar experience, she felt upset, furious and hugely betrayed. Also feeling very guilty, she continually lamented: "How could I have put you through this, when you yourself must have been so sad?" I replied that I was glad that I had had the opportunity to give her this gift–helping her move through this process just as my previous therapist had done with me. Although I would never have chosen to share this significant piece of my life with her (in general, I don't reveal personal information to patients), this transaction became a fortuitous vehicle for critical movement in her therapy with me. Seeing that I, too, was vulnerable and experienced deep sadness in my life, she could then accept that she could be less than perfect as well.

My personal experiences, covering the full spectrum of life's bounty, both positive and negative, have informed my therapy with patients. I can identify with what it's like to sit in my patient's chair, feeling overwhelmed with the journey that lies ahead. I can identify and empathize, in a very real sense, with my patients' pain. I know what illness and sudden death look like. I know the face of alcoholism and denial. I know the importance of clear boundaries in families and what happens when they are inappropriately open or closed. I know what family dysfunction looks like and how healthy families should function. I know the power of family patterns and the far-reaching tentacles they are likely to produce over generations. I know what it is like to mourn, to be emotionally alone, clinically depressed, anxious and angry. Through the strength and resources I have come to know in myself, I look for those in my patients–excavating, respecting and encouraging their survival skills. As one of my patients expressed so eloquently in a letter to me: "I am so thankful for your tolerance, patience and your optimism. I look forward to the day that I can own it all for myself without feeling like I need you to hold it for me."

My passage and those of my patients have mutually impacted on each other. In my interactions with my patients, I recognize what I preach but don't practice, encouraging me to change my behavior as well. My patients continually remind me of my strengths as well as my weaknesses. Most importantly, their success stories have amplified my hope in a better, happier present and future for mankind and myself. I have experienced incredible heights of pride, caring and positive energy in my collaboration with my patients, as we empower each other. I am eternally grateful for the lessons we have taught each other through the years, as we continually evolve our protean selves.

In closing, I'd like to share with you a beautiful poem, a treasured gift, composed by one of my patients, who has chosen to remain anonymous (She has graciously given me permission to publish it):

> We wander together
> To explore the caves
> Darkness envelops me
> She sees points of light
> Ways to escape
> To embody the freedom
> That can eternally exist
> Without completeness
> Without perfection
> Sunshine burns if you get too much
> She says.
> Accept
> Enjoy

Stay in the cave as long as you need
And I'll continue to lead you
   To those
      Few
         But powerful
            Points of light.

REFERENCE

Tessler, Nancy (1994). The other part of me. *The Family Therapy Networker*, 45.

The Radical Leap of True Empathy:
A Case Example

Maryhelen Snyder

SUMMARY. Empathic capacity is widely considered to be a primary ingredient of intimacy. In the couple case described here, the partners had revealed considerable competence in empathic attunement to one another when the issues were somewhat removed from their own deepest sensitivities. A critical incident had occurred a number of years prior to therapy that was processed by the couple in two sessions which are described in this article. These sessions reveal the complexities and significance of the empathic leap when one's own emotions are intensely involved. I asked the couple to read this article and to include their perceptions of the sessions described. *[Article copies available for a fee from The Haworth Document Delivery Service: 1-800-342-9678. E-mail address: <getinfo@haworthpressinc.com> Website: <http://www.HaworthPress.com>]*

KEYWORDS. Empathy, couples, communication

By definition and etiology, intimacy requires access to the inmost experience of the other person and the ability to share one's own inmost experience. The wife in the case example given here had been raped by an uncle when she was a child, and physically abused by her father.

Maryhelen Snyder, PhD, is a Couple and Family Therapist in Albuquerque, NM. She is the Clinical Director of the New Mexico Relationship Enhancement Institute and adjunct faculty in the Departments of Psychology and Psychiatry at the University of New Mexico.

[Haworth co-indexing entry note]: "The Radical Leap of True Empathy: A Case Example." Snyder, Maryhelen. Co-published simultaneously in *Journal of Couples Therapy* (The Haworth Press, Inc.) Vol. 9, No. 3/4, 2000, pp. 97-111; and: *The Personhood of the Therapist* (ed: Barbara Jo Brothers) The Haworth Press, Inc., 2000, pp. 97-111. Single or multiple copies of this article are available for a fee from The Haworth Document Delivery Service [1-800-342-9678, 9:00 a.m. - 5:00 p.m. (EST). E-mail address: getinfo@haworthpressinc.com].

During her own therapy on sexual abuse, she had experienced an incident with her husband in which she felt raped by him, and had said so at the time with considerable fury and anguish. Each person's inmost experience during this incident had remained hidden from the other.

AN OVERVIEW OF EMPATHIC PROCESS

Martin Buber understood that the actual step into the lifeworld of another human being requires the "deepest stirring of one's being" (1988; p. 71). Considerable research as well as personal experience reveals the ways in which, on the side of positive affect, this empathic capacity reveals itself as wonder and love, and, on the side of negative affect, it may reveal itself as something akin to terror and the experience of loss. Buber prefers the word "inclusion" to the word "empathy" (1957) because of his strong emphasis on how a person who is engaging in intimate relationship must not forfeit the felt reality of his/her experience while at the same time living through the event from the standpoint of the other. The listener doesn't lose the "I" in the process of experiencing the "Thou." I have written about empathic process elsewhere (see Snyder 1995; 1996). I would also recommend Bugenthal and Sterling (1993) and Friedman (1976; 1985), in addition to Buber for in-depth explorations of this subject.

In the domain of psychotherapy and the wider domain of communication, what goes by the name of empathy often falls short of the radical leap into the experience of "the other." This failure in understanding the nature of empathy is sometimes used to underestimate or discredit empathy itself as a therapeutic process. The blocks to full empathy are legion and perhaps the most subtle, and at times insidious, is the assumption that one is being empathic when one is not. The expert on whether empathy is accurate or not is the person who is the recipient of empathy. The face of someone who receives empathy at a depth that goes beyond what they have as yet been able to express or even "know," or beyond what they have found fully acceptable in their own experience, is usually an almost instant register of the degree of adequacy of empathic attunement.

HISTORY OF COUPLE WORK

Tony and Elizabeth (names and some details disguised to protect anonymity) have been married for approximately 30 years. Their three adult children no longer live at home. Prior to coming to me for couple therapy (approximately two years ago), they had taken a class given by myself and a colleague on "Relationship Enhancement Skills" (Guerney, 1977; Snyder, 1991). Since that time, they have come to therapy sessions together, and occasionally separately, to address relationship issues approximately once a month, and have also participated in two couple groups led by myself and the same colleague with whom I taught the class.

What stands out for me most dramatically in my work with them is their interest in not settling for a level of intimacy, self-awareness, or conscious living that feels less than what might be possible. At the same time, as will be evidenced below, they are occupied, as perhaps most of us are in this culture, in striving for these possibilities as goals to be achieved within the framework of a view of human beings (self and other) as either acceptable or not acceptable.

As with many couples of their generation, they began their relationship with what probably appeared to others, and to some degree appeared to them, as a relatively high level of intimacy within the context of traditional roles. First of all, the sexual attraction between them was strong. Tony had experienced a substantial number of sexual relationships prior to marriage; Elizabeth was a virgin. They both remember their sexual experience on their wedding night as one that was deeply satisfying. Elizabeth then took on the traditional role of wife as homemaker, cook, sexual partner, and mother. Tony was extremely busy with his job, which demanded considerable travel. When he returned home at the end of a busy day or from his periods away, he was often eager to make love. Elizabeth found that she felt decreasingly responsive at these times and that Tony didn't seem to notice. She pretended more responsiveness than she felt, and her occasional attempts to be authentic about what she wanted and what she missed in the relationship, sexual or otherwise, seemed to her to meet with resistance or indifference. In retrospect, if not at that time, Tony is aware that he has felt a deep desire to perform well in virtually every aspect of his life, and, in fact, that his self respect has depended on this performance. When confronted with Elizabeth's unhappiness, and particularly when this unhappiness has been communicated in a way that felt critical, he has responded at times with denial, anger, counter-criticalness, and distance. It would probably be accurate to say that Elizabeth has responded to Tony's attempts to share his feelings in similar ways. In other ways as well, they share in the cultural complexities of communication; the myriad ways in which feelings are spoken and/or heard in a manner that evokes shame and the defenses against shame.

When Elizabeth entered individual and group therapy ten years ago because of her growing awareness that her early abuse experiences had profoundly affected her ability to value herself, Tony attended some sessions with her. In one session that was particularly devastating for him, his experience was that he was being told by his wife and the therapist that he had been a bad husband, insensitive to his wife's sexual vulnerabilities and needs. He felt that he was being told that he was one of her abusers. Shortly after this he attended a weekend retreat for men at which he felt emotionally safe enough to grieve his feelings of being wrongly accused of this much insensitivity. This period was both exciting and difficult for Elizabeth because she felt as though many of her painful experiences were being voiced for the first time and being validated in therapy. She wanted Tony to understand the significance of this in her life and to support her growing abilities to notice what she wanted and to speak openly about it. Tony did some considerable growing of his own at this time, largely through addressing the "workaholic" manifestations of his need to perform well. He participated, and has continued to participate, in a "twelve-step program" that has helped him look more honestly at the ways in which his need to be seen as performing well has interfered with his ability to listen to his own needs as well as the needs of others.

Therapy sessions (and group therapy sessions) with Elizabeth and Tony have been satisfying experiences, for the most part, for all three of us. They have seemed to be unusually motivated and competent in listening to each other carefully, and have clearly been interested in having a deeply authentic and intimate relationship. We have audiotaped virtually all the sessions and they have usually listened to these audiotapes between sessions. At the same time, it appeared to all of us that some level of mutual trust continued to be missing. They both agreed that they tended to avoid the kind of conversations at home that they had in my office, and they also reported how sometimes when they attempted to be open with each other in this way, they each felt quickly blamed and shamed. Tony reported that the tension he felt in this relationship at times was, in his view, taking a toll on his physical health, and that he longed for the "way it used to be" in the early years when he rested assured that he was loved, desired, and appreciated.

Elizabeth felt that if Tony remained unwilling to get individual therapy for himself, he might always be unable to listen and respond to her in the way she most deeply desired. In the few months preceding the sessions that will be described below, Elizabeth had decided that she would not continue to make love with Tony unless a substantial change occurred in that part of their relationship. In her view, in spite of everything which she felt she had attempted to tell him about her needs for more relating prior to and during love making, as well as more openness on his part to her expressions of what she needed in order to be sexually satisfied, he continued to make love with her on his own terms. During this time, their friendship actually grew deeper in certain ways. Elizabeth had determined to show Tony the love she felt for him (as well as the attraction) and she found this easier to do when she was being honest and firm about not making love in the old way. They almost always went to sleep at night holding each other. Tony commented that his body seemed to be handling this requirement for celibacy by not getting aroused. In the context of group therapy, he reported that it felt like a great loss to him not to be using this "cylinder," but that he didn't feel he knew how at this point to give Elizabeth what she needed. Once when he thought she was aroused and touched her breast, she had described what he had done as "groping." She discovered during this period that she was feeling increasingly sexual. She wrote erotic poems and at one point shared some of her writing with Tony. He told her he had difficulty trusting its authenticity. It was clear that their feelings of being blamed and shamed were accurate reflections of what was actually happening. The fact that it was happening in relatively subtle ways made it more difficult for each of them to see themselves doing it, even though they never failed to experience the receiving end of these subtle forms of judgment.

Background to the Two Sessions Described Below

During the time that Elizabeth was receiving intensive therapy about ten years ago for her early abuse experiences she had not wanted to make love with Tony. One night she had taken two anti-histamine pills for a bad cold and had fallen into an especially deep sleep. Before going to sleep, she had, as she remembers it, reiterated her strong desire not to make love. At the same time she had felt a desire to be held by Tony for nurture and comfort. She was naked, as she often chose to be in bed, and he held her in the "spoon" position in which they often fell asleep. In the middle of the night she awoke and discovered that she felt moisture between her legs. When she went into the bathroom to check what it was, she discovered that Tony had ejaculated and assumed that he had also had intercourse with her as she slept deeply. She felt (as she reported later in the session described below) both panic and rage. She went back into their room and accused him angrily of having sex with her against her wishes; in fact, of "raping" her. This memory was similar in most respects for both Elizabeth and Tony. Each had a strong residue of unresolved emotions from that night, and they had never been able to successfully speak with each other about them.

METHODOLOGY OF THERAPY

In therapy sessions, Elizabeth and Tony had been using the method of "becoming" the other person that I have found, and clients have found, to be an unusually powerful tool for helping people to take the empathic leap when their own emotions or viewpoints are both strong and in partial opposition to the emotions and perspective of the other person. I have written about this method in greater depth than I can do here (Snyder 1995). It is similar in some respects to the psychodramatic techniques of "role reversal" and "doubling" (Moreno 1947), to techniques of "identification" and "becoming" that Guerney (1987) uses in the Relationship Enhancement Therapy he developed, to the technique that Tomm (1992) has called "interviewing the other in the self," and to a supervision technique developed by Bugenthal and Sterling (1993). The method of "becoming" creates by most reports an ability to deeply understand the experience of another person that one doesn't realize one had available to consciousness. I have personally observed, for example, that whenever, as a therapist, I am feeling an impasse in the therapeutic process (with the frequent concomitant aspects of confusion and criticalness), I can request my clients' permission to attempt to speak from their perspective. In doing this, I may, as Bugenthal and Sterling (1993) observe, encounter some internal resistance's to feeling fully what my client might be feeling, but if I risk moving past these resistances and feeling whatever I might have to feel in doing so, both I and my client typically discover that more empathic accuracy is available to me than I have realized, and that this empathic accuracy dissolves the therapeutic impasse.

Tony and Elizabeth have discovered the same reality. But they have also discovered something else, which Elizabeth articulated clearly in the first of the two sessions described below: that one can fake the "becoming" and not even be fully conscious that one is doing that until one stops doing it.

Unfortunately, the first of the two sessions described below was neither audio-taped nor video-taped. I have had to re-construct it from notes and memory, with assistance from Elizabeth and Tony. The second session was video-taped in its entirety, so I have been able to transcribe some parts of it. Each of these sessions created a major shift in the couple's understanding of the experience of making the empathic leap into the lifeworld of the other.

FIRST SESSION:
ELIZABETH'S EXPERIENCE OF THE SHIFT FROM SELF TO OTHER

In this session, the choice was made for both Elizabeth and Tony to share as fully as they could their factual and emotional memories of the night described above when Elizabeth had accused Tony of raping her.

After each person spoke of their experience, the other one would reflect it back using the method of "becoming" to go as deeply as possible into understanding the experience of the other.

Elizabeth spoke first. She described with considerable affect how the experience of waking up groggy and discovering the sperm between her legs was extremely reminiscent of the experience of being sexually assaulted by her uncle as a little girl. She had been too young at the time to know exactly what was happening. What she spoke to Tony about at this session was the experience of discovering the sperm between her legs after he had ejaculated against her, and the panic she felt at that time. Part of the trauma was that when she told her mother about this experience, her mother told her she "must have deserved it." She felt that as a result of that message, and the way in which it is culturally compounded by messages from men that the desirability of women makes them responsible for what is done to them, her self-doubt was triggered that night with Tony. Her fury was compounded by the injustice of that message even though Tony had not given the message at that time.

Tony then spoke as Elizabeth. At certain points I assisted him in going more deeply into the experience. I think Tony and Elizabeth will concur that at this session he did a fairly good job of accurately reflecting what she remembered feeling that night (and still felt), but it wasn't until the following session that he grasped her experience at the deepest level. Toward the end of this session, Tony spoke at one point of a certain confusion he felt in understanding the depth of fear and rage that Elizabeth seemed to feel. At this moment, I became Elizabeth and spoke of the experience of betrayal as a young child that occurs when "I" am innocently, trustingly feeling close to the person who then sexually abuses me. I also expressed how different it might have been if "I" had been able to talk with somebody about it, but instead I was supposed to forget the actual experience of what happened. I cried as I spoke this in the session. Elizabeth felt accurately understood and cried as well, and Tony's face and words reflected that he felt some clarification of why the experience had such an impact on Elizabeth.

Before this clarification took place, however, Elizabeth felt satisfied enough with the empathic accuracy which Tony had shown to say that she could listen to his memories of that night. Tony spoke of how close he had felt to her holding her naked body in his arms. When he had an erection as he almost always did when he was this close to her, he didn't feel that she would be troubled if he simply rubbed himself between her legs and ejaculated. He did not have intercourse with her, and believed that he was honoring her request. He spoke of how her request had been hard on him because of his desire and because he was receiving messages from her, her individual therapist, and her group therapist that he was insensitive as a husband in ways he didn't understand. He had also learned that the sexual satisfaction that Elizabeth had seemed to feel in the early years of their relationship had been pretended by her. He felt that he could not talk openly with her about his own emotional pain. When she woke him up to accuse him of having raped her, he was shocked by the intensity of her emotions. He felt unfairly accused, hurt, and angry as a result.

As Elizabeth listened to Tony, she was clearly feeling intense emotions of her own. Her face was flushed and there were tears in her eyes. We had a brief conversation about how it might be somewhat difficult for her to step out of her own feelings, as it were, and into his, but she said she thought she could do it and would like to try. She then did something I had never seen done before. She found a way to contain her own feelings and Tony's alternately. First, she became Tony, doing an unusually sensitive job of experiencing this event from his perspective. He was clearly touched by her ability to understand, and kept nodding his head in affirmation that she was grasping how this night had felt to him. As she did this, her face did not reveal her own emotions until at a certain point one could see them beginning to surface again. At this point, she said, "Excuse me just a minute," and turning to one side she began to sob for one or two minutes while Tony and I waited quietly. She then turned back to him, with a face clear of her own feelings, and said, "Okay, I can become you again now." Again she became Tony with sensitivity and accuracy. When she was finished, he thanked her. I asked him then if he could speak to Elizabeth about how it had felt to him to be understood in this way. He cried as he told her how moving this experience was.

We then discussed what had happened to Elizabeth when she did this. She spoke of her growing awareness that very often when she had been empathizing with Tony in the past, she had been holding on to some degree to her own perspective and feeling some reservations or judgments about his experience, even while empathizing accurately. She felt that in this session, she didn't allow herself that indulgence; that she had determined to understand him all the way. Because of this, she had spontaneously invented a way to deal with her own feelings when they arose with such intensity that she could not stay fully with Tony for a moment. What interested all of us was how short-lived this break from empathy had been and how well it had worked.

Between this session and the next, Tony and Elizabeth made love. Elizabeth commented that it had been very useful to think of it as play. In a session prior to the one described above, Elizabeth had come alone because Tony was out of town. My recollection of this session is that she and I both "became" Tony at various points in the session and that a core awareness for Elizabeth that resulted from this session is how much her focus on Tony not doing things right (e.g., making love right, doing his own therapeutic work right, relating right) fed his already existing anxieties about not performing adequately. Bringing the concept of playfulness to their love making released her, and therefore him, from this task orientation to life. It made room for bumbling. This, combined, with Tony and Elizabeth's feelings that they were understanding and forgiving each other more fully, seemed to provide the door back into their sexual intimacy.

SECOND SESSION:
TONY'S DISTINCTION
BETWEEN ACCEPTANCE AND FIXING

This session began with Elizabeth's inquiry into the question of "amends" which is a strong point of focus in the twelve-step programs. She wondered whether focus on one's own hurt feelings could sometimes make the other person responsible for one's well being, and could detract from the usefulness of giving attention to how one has hurt others rather than emphasizing how others have hurt us. Tony's inquiry was addressed primarily to me; he wanted something of a progress report from me on how they were doing individually and relationally. Both inquiries were useful, and reflective of critical process. Tony had observed his own sense of movement, and was aware on reflection of how much he had been conditioned to make progress in order to arrive somewhere where he could feel okay as a human being. Much of the couple work is a mutually dialogic process of de-constructing assumptions such as this one (that one must make progress in order to be okay) that are culturally pervasive.

I asked Elizabeth whether she would like to talk with Tony about amends that she wanted to make to him. She spoke to him of her sorrow for having projected onto him anger and mistrust that really belonged to earlier relationships in her life.

When he "became" her, he didn't catch her realization of how she had intentionally hurt him. She corrected him, "I *did* want to hurt you . . . because I was hurting so bad."

In the second part of the session Tony spoke to Elizabeth about his new awareness of the actuality of how much she had been hurt by early sexual and physical abuse, and of how he had been insensitive to that pain. He said, "I wasn't listening. And I was hiding my own needs. You were vulnerable and very tender. I came on strong and violated your desire not to have sex. I realize the pain that I caused you."

For the first time in the history of their relationship, Elizabeth experienced that Tony actually understood what had happened to her and why she had reacted so intensely that night she accused him of rape. As he spoke to her, she cried quietly. We decided that it was less important to reflect back what she had heard than to share her response. She said, "I don't know what to say. It felt very sincere; you understood. . . . There was a shift in my perception that started in our last session. I felt less crazy after learning how it was for you. All this has changed my pain, taken it away. As important an event as it was, now that we've talked about it, it seemed unimportant. The sting has gone out of it."

In response, Tony said, "I'm seeing, regardless of what my intentions were, what it must have been like for you." They gave each other a long hug, and Elizabeth spoke playfully of how he could now make nothing but mistakes for the rest of the week and this one gift he had given her would keep her loving and forgiving him.

In this same session, Tony told me that he felt a new awareness of how it might be for a woman, such as his daughter, if she got raped. He cried as he spoke of how that would be "a life time burden" for a woman, an experience that "would affect a woman's perception of everything from then on." I agreed, but I also verified with Elizabeth my understanding of her recent experience that once she felt fully understood by Tony, her experience of abuse and betrayal lost its "charge."

When Elizabeth said "Yes," Tony cried again and said, "I've been fighting all my life being blamed for someone else's transaction,–not wanting to feel her pain, to take on the guilt,–not listening. I was afraid I'd feel it as a burden, that I'd have to go out and do something."

I spoke of how the something he was doing right now, in listening at a very deep level, made a great difference. "Years ago," Tony said, "a therapist said to me, 'Can you imagine the fear that women feel walking across a parking lot?' and I said, 'Bull shit; I don't do things like that.' I couldn't hear it."

ELIZABETH'S COMMENTS

My intense feelings of violation and fear from both my childhood and the recent incident with my husband, had created a wall of defense and very little trust. No matter how much we talked and empathized about other issues, avoiding this one made the possibility of a deeper intimacy only a desire and not a reality.

The experience of feeling fully understood and visible in my pain when Tony empathized and then when he agreed that the incident that had occurred between us was indeed similar in nature to what had happened to me as a child, made an enormous difference to us as a couple and also to me in the continuation of my healing from both the sexual abuse and my mother's denial.

I don't believe that I could have reached down and empathized on such an emotional issue, if I had not worked on establishing a clearer sense of myself through individual therapy. I was able to hold the wounded part of me, somewhere around twelve years old and still go deeply into the experience from Tony's perspective. This container of myself is useful when I am experiencing intense emotion.

I had a deep and certain desire to understand Tony and what he had experienced that night. I wanted to resolve some of the pain between us in order to make room for more intimacy. But I want to emphasize how much it seemed to me that my ability to listen at a very deep level depended on my ability to "hold" myself with great tenderness and self-protectiveness. Taking time to cry while I was listening to Tony was part of this ability I experienced to "hold" us both.

The outcome of being seen and heard for both of us created a level of trust that has promoted more honesty and also much more playfulness.

TONY'S COMMENTS

I eventually came to the realization, after numerous coaching sessions, that I had to set aside my own feelings and perceptions about the described events and experiences that were being expressed by Elizabeth. I frequently focused heavily on my own experiences of the same events while she was speaking, especially when those experiences and feelings were very different from Elizabeth's. I used to feel angry and betrayed by what I heard and frequently thought there were errors and exaggerations about the "chain of events" expressed by Elizabeth. When I set aside my feelings and perceptions for the moment, and paid maximum attention to what Elizabeth was saying and recognized that those were her truths, I was better able to empathize with her and delay the expression of my own truths until I was speaking.

The success of the therapeutic process for me has been learning the skill of listening to Elizabeth with my heart and empathizing with what she has said, despite what I sometimes perceived as inaccuracy and invalidity from my experience. Getting myself away from having to pass judgment on what Elizabeth is sharing, and trying to sincerely

*believe in her expressed reality, as she is talking, has been a break-
through for me. I have also found myself wanting to immediately reject
or criticize Elizabeth's reality if the same setting and events were not
what I experienced. I seem to be better able now to find the patience to
defer acknowledging my different feelings and perceptions while Elizabeth is talking. Afterwards, I can relatively quickly get in touch with
my feelings that surfaced while Elizabeth was sharing, but only after I
have fully empathized to her satisfaction.*

*When I was reading this article, I thought the cultural background
differences between us (both in ethnicity and in class) should be men-
tioned because I think they have had a strong effect on our marriage. I
also think that the word "compassion" would come closer to expressing what I feel rather than her word "attunement."*

DISCUSSION

Therapeutic process often reminds me of T. S. Eliot's often quoted
line about going all this way to get back to the beginning and know it
for the first time. There is increasing evidence from the research that
we are born with the capacity for deep empathic attunement, and that
our sense of our existence as human beings and our freedom to feel
what we feel, and perceive what we perceive, to trust our experience
and our intelligence is critically dependent on the empathic attunement
of primary care-takers. It is less clear I think how the factors that get in
the way of that attunement come into existence for human beings,
whether we are born with those impediments or whether they are
artifacts of culture and civilization. Central to what gets in the way is
the mind's tendency to defend its "self" internally and externally
from perspectives that appear to challenge its own world view, particularly if those perspectives imply in any way that we are wrong, bad,
or inferior. These messages of being wrong, bad, and inferior are
culturally pervasive as tools of "civilization" and socialization practiced by parents and society. We can certainly observe the patterns of
dominance in the entire biological structure of the world; human beings have incorporated those patterns into our communication practices. Those patterns invariably and inevitably induce shame and the
inhibition and constraint of consciousness.

We do, however, have evidence, that we can choose not to apply
these practices of dominance and subordination to relationships among

human beings, and to our internalized relationship with ourselves. The whole twelve step program, for example, is founded on the insight that the dominant/subordinate relationship with one's self in which one wills change and attempts to dominate and control one's impulses (and simultaneously evade that domination and control) sometimes doesn't work. What works is a shift in understanding the nature of the problem. The problem is no longer the problem; one's way of approaching the problem is the problem.

Elizabeth and Tony have taken major steps of understanding the nature of full empathy, the ease with which we block it, and the energy and courage it requires not to block it with practices of avoidance, indifference, argumentativeness, defensiveness, shaming, etc. It may be that "abstinence" from these practices, to borrow the twelve-step language, is a requirement of intimacy. As Elizabeth notes, however, certain practices of self-protection are essential to intimacy: we must be able to "hold" ourselves while "holding" the other.

Perhaps the most subtle layer of the conditioning that blocks intimacy is the whole construction of "self." The cultural/linguistic meaning of "self" is so conditioned into our thinking from birth on, that it becomes almost impossible to see beyond this "self" (like the proverbial example of the fish seeing beyond water) as we go about the daily business of living. It is very possible that what is called the "higher power" in the twelve-step program is simply the experience of referencing an awareness, intelligence, courage, and love that is not bound up in our cultural assumptions about "self" as the source of awareness, knowledge, and action.

In summary then, I think that Elizabeth and Tony now have the capacity to step fully into the lifeworlds of the other person when they so choose. This capacity developed from the distinctions they have been able to make between feeling empathic and not feeling empathic. They have noticed the ways in which they can hold on to their own perspectives (analyses, judgments, etc.) in subtle ways while going through the motions of empathic attunement, and they have noticed how it feels not to do that. In making this distinction, the human being steps into a quality of consciousness that is radically different from that in which "self" and "other" are experienced as separate phenomena.

REFERENCES

Buber, M. (1957). *Pointing the way: Selected essays.* (M.S. Friedman, trans. and ed.) New York: Harper & Row.

Buber, M. (1988). *The knowledge of man: Selected essays.* (M.S. Friedman & R.G. Smith, trans.) Atlantic Highlands, NJ: Humanities Press.

Bugenthal, J. & Sterling, M. (1993). The meld experience in psychotherapy supervision. *Journal of Humanistic Psychology* 33: 38-48.

Friedman, M.S. (1976). *Martin Buber: The Life of Dialogue.* Chicago and London: The University of Chicago Press.

Friedman, M.S. (1985). *The Healing Dialogue in Psychotherapy.* New Jersey: Jason Aronson, Inc.

Guerney, B.G., Jr. (1987). *Relationship Enhancement: Marital/family therapist manual.* State College, PA: IDEALS.

Moreno, J.L. (1947). *The theatre of spontaneity.* Beacon, New York: Beacon House.

Snyder, M. (1991). The Relationship Enhancement model of family therapy: A systematic eclectic approach: *Journal of Family Psychotherapy, 2,* 1-26.

Snyder, M. (1995). "Becoming": A method for expanding systemic thinking and deepening empathic accuracy. *Family Process, 34* (2), 241-253.

Tomm, K. (1992). *Interviewing the internalized other.* Workshop presented at the American Association of Marriage and Family Therapy, Amelia Island, FL.

When Illness Intrudes

Karen D. Fergus

SUMMARY. The author describes the impact of illness on her own intimate relationship, and discusses ways these personal experiences have influenced her psychotherapy practice with couples and individuals in the area of psychosocial oncology. Standard psychological classifications are overlaid on top of her personal narrative in order to highlight the differences between nomothetic and idiographic modes of description and representation, and to demonstrate the inherent limitations of the former in clinical practice. *[Article copies available for a fee from The Haworth Document Delivery Service: 1-800-342-9678. E-mail address: <getinfo@ haworthpressinc.com> Website: <http://www.HaworthPress.com>]*

KEYWORDS. Illness, narrative, couples, couples therapy

It is true that psychiatrists and clinical psychologists have long known that they should take the patient's own story as a starting point. But almost immediately they redact this story into general categories, dismembering the complex pattern of life into standard dimensions . . . (Allport, 1962, p. 415).

Perhaps it is *our own* stories, however, that should be taken as the starting point, for they are the ones which will most profoundly influ-

Karen D. Fergus, MA, is Psychotherapist and Research Associate at the Toronto-Sunnybrook Regional Cancer Centre and is affiliated with York University, Toronto, Ontario.

Address correspondence to: Karen D. Fergus, Support Services, Toronto-Sunnybrook Regional Cancer Centre, 2075 Bayview Avenue, Toronto, Ontario M4N 3M5.

[Haworth co-indexing entry note]: "When Illness Intrudes." Fergus, Karen D. Co-published simultaneously in *Journal of Couples Therapy* (The Haworth Press, Inc.) Vol. 9, No. 3/4, 2000, pp. 113-124; and: *The Personhood of the Therapist* (ed: Barbara Jo Brothers) The Haworth Press, Inc., 2000, pp. 113-124. Single or multiple copies of this article are available for a fee from The Haworth Document Delivery Service [1-800-342-9678, 9:00 a.m. - 5:00 p.m. (EST). E-mail address: getinfo@haworthpressinc.com].

ence what we see in our clients, and how we approach them in therapy. In my current practice, I work with individuals and couples who have been touched by cancer in varying ways. I will therefore begin this paper with my own story of how illness has influenced my intimate relationships and personal evolution. I will then go on to describe the ways in which I feel my personal story affects my clinical work.

In the spirit of Allport's cogent assertion, I will purposefully apply the categories we have created in the discipline of psychosocial oncology, and more broadly, health and family psychology, to my own story. My intention is to demonstrate, by way of contrast, just how far removed these categories are from the multi-dimensionality of experience. Although the parceling of life in the nomothetic tradition may help to ease our understanding of the highly intricate nature of human beings and relationships, we should not deceive ourselves into believing that we have grasped our clients' experiences on the basis of *our* categorical systems. We have only succeeded in packaging them–in our language, on our terms, in ways that are primarily helpful to us as professionals. Contrasting a professional stance with my personal narrative has made me acutely aware of the limitations of applying a standardized body of knowledge to my own work with individuals and couples.

THE AFTERSHOCK OF ILLNESS

It was a cold morning in February, a few days after their mother had died. Raymond had long since fled the house to go play shinny hockey, alone. His younger brother, David, called up the stairs, "Karen, will you come draw with me?" Ken was still asleep. He had come home late the past few nights, commuting between Toronto and Mississauga where his sons used to live and his ex-wife, Sher, was hospitalized. Two weeks ago she had gone in for "more tests." A month ago, Ken had torn his eight and eleven year old sons out of their home, their school, and the neighborhood that they had lived in all their lives. Seemingly overnight, he had assembled two bunk beds and a chest of drawers in the spare room. His forte–battening down the hatches. A crisis was about to happen. Or were we in the midst of one?

I pick myself up out of bed, go downstairs and pull out the green, tin box of pencil crayons. On the table there rests a hibiscus plant with a single, vibrant red blossom, decidedly watching over David who is hovered over a piece of paper. David is drawing a shark in Lake Ontario, hard, jagged lines, red over top of black. I think that this is his first rendering after the loss of his mother, and make a mental note to keep it for him for when he's older. With a lead pencil he begins forming chaotic smears and dark rings around his shark. "What's that?" I ask. "It's pollution," he exclaims, "You can't draw Lake Ontario without some pollution!" An unvoiced reply runs through my mind, "Yeah, life really stinks doesn't it." It was a comment about my own life as much as his.

Family Reorganization

The reality of Sher's pending death had hit Ken and I hard. Perhaps up until the moment that we allowed ourselves to consider her as dying, we had shrouded ourselves in our own form of denial, wanting to believe she would live, be miraculously cured. At least from my end, it was a denial born of selfishness, that Ken and I could ensure our existence as a couple separate from his life as a father. Having the kids on weekends and holidays was fine, even fun sometimes, but full-time felt to me like an invasion, plain and simple. The day the covers of denial had been lifted, we wandered around the city, aimlessly, wondering what would come of "us," would we make it through. Ken wondered if I would stay in the relationship. I wondered if I could handle staying in the relationship. Together, nothing seemed to comfort us. We stood downtown, in a haze of despondence, unable to decide if we wanted to distract ourselves by going to see a movie.

I rang Sher in the hospital, the morning of her death. She answered the phone sounding hoarse and weak. When I told her that I wanted to visit, she became flustered and asked to speak to Ken. I heard him console her, "Don't worry she'll understand. No one is going to be upset with you. No, you aren't being mean." Any sentimental fantasy I had conjured in my mind of her parlaying words of wisdom to me, the woman who would carry on with her two children, in an intimate and final good-bye, was not going to happen. As one who thrives on resolution, I would quickly have to learn to do without it. However, I did find comfort in other things: Knowing she had made it explicit that Karen was to receive her fuchsia sheets, (we both shared a penchant for flannelette bedding), and seeing a single bud appear, and start to flower, on the long dormant hibiscus plant shortly after she died.

I was out that evening when the expectant message was left on the answering machine. Ken and the boys would be spending the night in Mississauga at his mother's, and he would be coming home the next day, with his sons, for good. Awaiting the arrival of my new life, I fervently clean out the fridge and organize the cupboards. My mother accompanies me grocery shopping and together we stock the kitchen. On the surface, I appear to be engaged in a peculiar type of nesting process, but deep down, I am desperately attempting to impose some type of order on a situation that is completely out of my control.

Social Support

I had to coax my mother out of her house that day. My father had been fighting his own battle with lung cancer for the past two years, struggling to continue working amidst repeated chemo treatments, blood transfusions, and with supplemental oxygen. She is his primary caregiver and I am convinced he would have died long ago without her. He is becoming increasingly more dependent on her and she has become more fearful of leaving him alone. I have already expressed my concern that she is wearing herself down, sacrificing her own life for his. She has told me, unequivocally, that she would rather be doing this than not. I hear her and lay off. For once in my life, I listen to my mother.

When someone you love has cancer, futures hinge on test results. After hearing more bad news about my father, I awoke one morning crying with the realization that, if I was to have children of my own, my father would never know them. Ken's own father had died suddenly of a heart attack many years ago, and around this time, Ken said something to me which I found oddly reassuring. "You know," he started, "when you think of your father, and I think of mine, there's really no difference, even though yours is alive and mine isn't. I remember traveling with him, his sense of humor, his loud, hearty laughter. It's really no different from how you remember your father right now." For a brief period, he helped me shift my attention from what I would lose, to what I had, and I did find it helpful.

Between my father and the boys' mother, cancer had become as familiar to us as brushing our teeth. It had become a part of our way of life. Driving home from my parents' house one day, David asked me, "Why do people die of cancer?" I offer an analogy in reply, comparing the body to a city and the vital pathways and fluids in the body to roadways and vehicles in the city. "Cancer is like a roadblock that often comes out of nowhere. When a major intersection or enough roads become blocked, then the cars with people and the people with messages and deliveries can't get around. When no-one can get through to anyone else, the city starts to fall apart." He seems to understand, and I take quiet pride in my ability to answer a difficult question.

Some time later, David, squinting up at the sun, poses another question, "Why does the sun have no shadow?" I skip a beat and mentally stumble. I watch my mind do loops. He has presented me with a paradox that I cannot resolve intellectually, a koan. I hesitate, giving him enough time to fire another question at me, "Why do people have to die?" I take an emotional fall. There are no clever answers, but a few words do come slowly, faintly, "I really don't know."

"My mother won't be coming skating with us tonight because she's dead!" David blurts out with a smile on his face as we walk to the park to go skating with two kids from the neighborhood. Like a gunshot, his words fill the crisp, still air. They look at him, stunned. Ken quickly steps in and explains. The older friend turns to his younger sister, "Oh, I guess it's the smile when you feel sad kind of thing." Later that night, Ken has a talk with his sons about how people respond to the news of death and appropriate ways of communicating about their mother. But David has succeeded in beginning his new life; having pierced the world with his loss, he has made it real.

Role Definition

Seemingly everywhere I turn, "mother" is slapped in my face. At twenty-eight and absorbed in my studies, I am not ready to bear children of my *own*, let alone become a mother to two half-grown ones! I fail to find any suitable role for myself and settle on being an "adult friend." I ask the boys how do they address me to their friends. "I don't know," David shrugs, "I just call you 'Karen.'" Raymond says, "I call you 'my dad's girlfriend.'" Yes, I like it, one degree of separation–that, I can live with.

The mother of two neighborhood friends feels guilty because David has asked to call her "mom," and has made her a mother's day gift. I reassure her that I am glad David finds comfort in her as a mother. Underneath, I am more than glad, I am actually quite relieved. My response to the imposition of the mother label shifts over time, from fear to anger to annoyance to distance to expectation and finally, to acceptance–an acceptance, not of the role of mother, but of other people's need to label me as such. Eventually, it becomes apparent that within our new family circle, we implicitly understand what we mean to each other; the difficulty lies in trying to explain it to others.

Because of the limited array of available role categories, I learned to define myself by what I was not. Over time, I began to feel confident standing in that space between. In time, I did succeed in creating a position in which I was comfortable. I prefer to call it a "position" rather than a "role," because it is not a ready-made, add a little hot water and stir, way of being. This position has been custom designed by me, by the way I relate to each of the boys, and they to me, and is not fixed. A role is confining, a position is assumed. Even so, it is not a position that I can easily communicate to others; it is what I live day to day, not what I describe. Most important, I am grateful that Ken was always sensitive to my predicament, and patient enough not to jump to define me even though it would have made his life a whole lot easier if he had done just that.

The truth is, however, I could not have walked into the role of mother without having had to relinquish a large part of my own identity. Resentment became my gauge, my indicator that I had treaded beyond the bounds of my "position." No, I decided early on, I will not do the boys' dishes while they watch The Simpsons. The boys did not like hearing that Ken and I were too busy to do their dishes as well as our own. More change. They now do their own laundry as well. I have to rationalize to myself that they are not going to be irrevocably damaged by having to assume more responsibility than their friends. I hope that they learn early on, what I did not, that other people have lives and needs and that the world does not revolve around servicing their needs. That is the difference, I believe, between a mother and what I am. At that age, a mother is an extension of oneself, not a free-standing figure with a life of one's own. There is an advantage to our type of arrangement. We have a built in mechanism working against mutual exploitation and out of that, I hope, arises mutual respect.

Boundary Definition

Boundary definition is a process. Sometimes you have to create the dividing line, and other times you smack right up against the one you always had, but never knew was there.

When I was young, my parents' bed was like an extension of their body. The next best thing to being held in their arms, was to be snuggled up in their bed. The tone changes substantially, however, in a living arrangement such as mine. An entire book could probably be written about what becomes of the matrimonial bed when families are "blended." Of course, it had never occurred to me that *our* bed would become a family affair until one night I crawled in only to slide up against the remnants of a bag of potato chips. It was yet another reminder that the task of boundary definition was not complete.

Another episode comes to mind: It is late spring and school is out. I arrive home one day to find a half a dozen of the neighborhood kids gathered in the living room, riveted to the television screen. It is a beautiful day outside and they are watching a video. I feel myself growing increasingly exasperated as I scan the hangout my home has become. The oldest in the group looks up at me and smiles a hello. He is completely at home on my couch with his arm around his new "girlfriend." She glances up, offering a listless wave of her hand. Within a fraction of a second, my entire visual field is overtaken by an image of her two very dirty, bare feet planted firmly on *my* dhurrie rug! Obviously upset, I pull Raymond aside. He explains that Ken has asked Thom, the wayward musician from across the street, to "keep an eye on us." And thus began our foray into the organization of suitable childcare and the establishment of house rules.

LIVING NEAR ILLNESS

Not too long after we had settled into our new living arrangement, Ken's eyes began to deteriorate. He has been diabetic since he was fourteen and was diagnosed with moderate to severe retinopathy when we had first begun our relationship. Being diagnosed with retinopathy is fairly abstract until floaters start to appear in your vision–like spots on the windshield of a car, I'm told. The spots are the result of blood vessels detaching from the retina and bleeding. Sometimes, the bleeding stops on its own, and sometimes the vessels have to be cauterized through laser surgery in order to inhibit the blood flow. His doctor, one of the top opthamologists in Canada, had been monitoring him steadily for a number of years when his vision began to fail rapidly. It seemed that whenever the pressure around his eyes exceeded a certain level, another blood vessel would burst. Bending down to pick something up, or tie his shoe became a dangerous act, as did any type of physical exertion. Vigorous exercise is integral to Ken's physical and emotional well-being, as it is for many diabetics especially those with childhood onset diabetes. What was once a source of pleasure and vitality had now become forbidden.

Illness Intrusiveness

Up until this crisis, I had been sheltered from Ken's illness. He is remarkable in his ability to seamlessly incorporate his blood sugar management and insulin injections into his daily life. From time to time, I would awaken at an early hour as Ken, soaked in a damp, cold sweat, was getting out of bed because his sugar had dropped dangerously low. When his sugar was high, he became irritable, a feeling he describes as, "So claustrophobic, it makes my teeth itch." But these happenings were a part of Ken, as disruptive for me as my menstruation was for him. They certainly were not the effects of *illness*. Illness was an occurrence that stopped us dead in our tracks, something that prevented us from doing stuff we enjoyed, and *that* had never been the case. We could do virtually anything we wanted including spending extended periods together in the backwoods of Ontario.

Anticipatory Grief

Every time a blood vessel burst, I imagined a pixel burning out on our life together. All of my forced choice complexes were triggered. What will happen if Ken goes blind? What will happen if he dies? Who will assume responsibility for the kids?!? Who else but Ken could keep up with the boys' intensive and time consuming hockey schedule? *Who else would want to?* I catch myself staring at the new duvet cover on our bed. The pattern reminds me of intertwined blood vessels–pink ones, blue ones, green ones. "Maybe I should get rid of it," I muse, "Maybe it's a bad omen."

Communication Problems

"How are his eyes today," I wonder, but dare not bring it up. Perhaps once every so often, but certainly not every time I think of it. I need not inflict my obsessional nature on him. Acute sensitivity replaces open communication. I don't really have to ask, I know: By the way he shuts the door at the end of the day; by the way he says hello on the other end of the phone line. I know. Despite the break-down in communication, we are indeed communicating. I experience his withdrawal but it is different from the cold, stonewalling after an argument; this is more of a quite, slipping away. I notice his right eye become lazy and lose its focus. Each time I look into his face, I am reminded of his reality, my reality. But we cannot speak of it.

I begin to feel isolated and terribly alone. The tension crescendos one evening into a memorable hollering match. "I need to know what you're going through. I can't be here if you're going to shut me out! I simply can't go on like this on my own. I need you to go through this with me or else I won't be able to go through this at all!" Am I threatening to leave him? I wonder. He charges back at me, "I'm doing everything I can to hold things together! Do you think this is easy? I'm facing my own death!"

And then one day I looked up at him, and there was no more life left in that right eye. I swear to this day, the blue of his iris had turned to gray.

I drove home from cottage country that weekend. Ken normally cannot stand it when I drive. He claims he gets car sick unless he is in control, but on that night, I know, he was grateful that I drove. We all afforded ourselves a bit of comic relief by playing an idiotic game where we tried to invent movie titles and advertising captions. Teeter-ing on the edge of sanity, I laughed myself into tears.

BEING WITH ILLNESS

Thanks to modern technology, a masterful opthamologist, and the unfoldment of a profound personal teaching in relation to his illness, Ken's eyesight was restored. When Ken's illness intruded on our life together, I was afforded a glimpse of his reality. I learned about the two worlds in which he resides: The world of raising two sons, of working, teaching, loving. And the world of the body. He has had to take over, where a vital organ left off. As someone who is reminded of his mortal-ity by four pricks of the needle a day, Ken does not dwell on illness. In fact, he finds it hard to imagine how I can do the work that I do.

He is not alone. It is not uncommon for clients to break away from their own reflexive process, only to home in on me, and question how

I am able to cope personally in this profession. I never really know how to respond. Perhaps I can do this work, not because I have experienced firsthand what it is like *to be* seriously ill, but because I have experienced firsthand what it is like to *be with* people who are. My clinical work accords with who I already am. It is not a matter of "leaving my work behind" or ensuring that "I don't take my work home with me," because "work" and "me" are not separate. Just as I cannot choose to take with, or leave behind, my sense of smell, or my right arm, I cannot separate myself from what I do.

For myself, *being with* as a psychotherapist involves more than empathic attunement and a handful of applied techniques. It entails confronting my own fears about illness and death, loss and abandonment, time and time again. I do not think it is possible to work and be with people who have life-threatening disease, without at some point, having to face one's own existential plight. Counselman (1997) describes the existential struggle she undergoes when the woman of a couple she had begun to see for a routine course of marital therapy is diagnosed with a recurrence of breast cancer. The woman is around the same age as she. Her client's question of "Why me?" is paralleled by her own, inward, "Why *not* me?" I sometimes think, "When me?" Professional distances are more difficult to assume when faced with matters of mortality.

My personal experiences with people who are ill have given me an appreciation for the haphazard ways in which illness unfolds. In psychooncology, we speak of "illness trajectories" and "disease progression" as though illness was a linear sequence of events. However, this is the illusion of the healthy professional, not the reality of a sick person. When you live with or near illness you quickly learn that illness has its own course, and that healing, when it does occur, occurs in mysterious ways. You are ultimately not in charge. My experience with illness has been like watching a foreboding cloud follow you around for days and days on end, sometimes even years. Then, one day, without warning, you find yourself seeking refuge from a raging hailstorm. Often, there is no time for reason or reasonable solutions because once illness takes hold, you no longer inhabit a world of reason, of prediction, control, and neat and tidy endings. You are expending all of your energy just trying to stay afloat. I would imagine that for the people I work with, sometimes reason can be very helpful, shedding light in dark places, and at other times, it must seem just plain invalidating.

In working therapeutically with couples where one person is sick, I have found it helpful to explicitly acknowledge that they are in the midst of a crisis. When I say this, I am not merely stating the obvious. The relational strife I encounter is often due to an unacknowledged assumption that life should be carrying on as it was before partners were caught in the stranglehold of illness. Although the context has changed substantially, often the partners themselves have not yet caught up to the changes that have occurred in their relationship. The track has taken a 180 degree turn, but the trolley is still headed in the same direction. I find that the resistance to the change is usually just as painful and devastating for the couple as the change itself.

If I had to identify a particular value that carries over from my personal story into my clinical practice, it is the value that illness affords with it the opportunity for individual change and growth, and the opportunity to draw couples closer together. The taking of one another for granted is much more difficult when the existence of one partner, and thus the entirety of the relationship, is being threatened. In my own relationship, the shared experience of illness has undoubtedly been a source of greater mutual appreciation, personal enrichment, and a deepened respect for one another. However, this outcome is predicated upon each partner's willingness, on some level, to meet the challenges that accompany the illness and to communicate about their struggle. I suspect that the reconstitution of the relationship is rarely had without a period of intense conflict as roles get juggled about, responsibilities are unmet, and needs go unfulfilled.

AFTERWARD

It is mid-August, over three years have passed since the boys moved in with us, and two years since the crisis with Ken's eyes. Ken knows I have spent the last couple of days hibernating upstairs in our den. I have given him a vague indication that I am writing about us, but he does not seem at all perturbed by the prospect. In fact, he jested with me about changing the names to protect the innocent. I figure, in all fairness, that he should have the chance to read through a paper about his life before it is submitted for publication. For the sake of time, I ask him to glance through it over dinner. After reading a few pages, he looks up at me, eyes moist and puts the paper aside. I start to feel anxious and wonder whether I expressed something he did not like. Where did I overstep my bounds? "It's good," he manages to say, "it's what I lived."

Having tested the broth too many times, I could no longer taste the soup. Now the taste of our story was interfering with Ken's dinner. Ken begins to eat again and I am eager to compare flashes of memory. I wonder if he recalls his phone conversation with Sher, the hollering match, his comforting words when my dad was dying. I come to the frightening realization that he is the only other person on this planet with whom I can validate these experiences. For a brief instant, I am able to stand outside of the relational space we have created within and between ourselves, and the rich, colorful world we co-inhabit. And look on with awe.

REFERENCES

Allport, G. W. (1962). The general and the unique in psychological science. *Journal of Personality, 30,* 405-422.

Counselman, E. F. (1997). Self-disclosure, tears and the dying client. *Psychotherapy, 34,* 233-237.

Index

AA (Alcoholics Anonymous), 33
Alcoholics Anonymous (AA), 33
Avanta Process Community I
See Process Community

Case example
See True empathy case example
Change artists, therapists as, 3
Connecting, 17-19
Couples therapy, integrity therapy
    perspective on
  counter-transference and
    acting out rate and, 39-40
    owning our shadows concept
      and, 38
    triad relationship and, 37,39
  discussion regarding, 38-40
  emotional involvement and, 33
  healing through, 40
  honesty and, 32
  integrity and, elements of, 32
  mental illness viewed by, 32
  philosophical perspective on
    choice between good and evil
      and, 31
    discovery of truth and, 31
    existential framework of, 30-31
    therapist/couple equality and,
      31-32
  responsibility and, 32-33
  summary regarding, 29-30
  theoretical basis of, 32-33
  therapist self-disclosure and
    boundaries and, 36,38
    consistency in level of, 34-35
    counsel *vs.* advice and, 33-34
    evaluative interview and, 35
    pre-commitment interview and,
      34-35

Twelve-step programs and, 33
value of, 33,38-40
vulnerability *vs.* strengths and, 37

"Dance of life" concept, 10
Day Top Village, 33
Disconnecting, 17-19

Equality in value of people, 11
Essential self of the therapist
  equality and uniqueness of people
    and, 11
  "freeze-framing" diagnosis
    concept and, 13
  harmony among people and, 12
  healing and heart energy and, 16-17
  healing potential within patient
    and, 2
  loving control and, 7-8
  personhood and categorizing and, 13
  personhood defined, 10-11
  position modes and, 7
  self worth awareness and, 2,47,59
  systems and
    how they work example, 3-7
    person's affect and having an
      effect, 12
    positive self-worth and, 14
    process in all systems and, 9-10
    therapist into family system and,
      7-9,18
  systems and how they work
    example, 9
  trust and, 1

Faces of the therapist
See Many faces of the therapist
Fergus, Karen D., 113

TO ORDER: CALL: 1-800-429-6784 / FAX: 1-800-895-0582 (outside US/Canada: + 607-771-0012) / **E-MAIL: getinfo@haworthpressinc.com**

☐ **YES**, please send me **The Therapist's Notebook**
___ $49.95 ISBN: 0-7890-0400-3. (Outside US/Canada/Mexico: $60.00)

- Individual orders outside US, Canada, and Mexico must be prepaid by check or credit card.
- Discounts are not available on 5+ text prices and not available in conjunction with any other discount.
- Discount not applicable on books priced under $15.00.
- 5+ text prices are not available for jobbers and wholesalers.
- Postage & handling: In US: $4.00 for first book, $1.50 for each additional book.
  Outside US: $5.00 for first book; $2.00 for each additional book.
- NY, MN, and OH residents: please add appropriate sales tax after postage & handling.
- Canadian residents: please add 7% GST after postage & handling.
- Payment in UNESCO coupons welcome.
- If paying in Canadian dollars, use current exchange rate to convert to US dollars.
- Please allow 3-4 weeks for delivery after publication.
- Prices and discounts subject to change without notice.

Signature _____

☐ **BILL ME LATER**($5 service charge will be added).
(Not available for individuals outside US/Canada/Mexico. Service charge is waived for/jobbers/wholesalers/booksellers.)
☐ Check here if billing address is different from shipping address and attach purchase order and billing address information.

☐ **PAYMENT ENCLOSED $** _____
(Payment must be in US or Canadian dollars by check or money order drawn on a US or Canadian bank.)

☐ **PLEASE BILL MY CREDIT CARD:**
☐ AmEx ☐ Diners Club ☐ Discover ☐ Eurocard ☐ JCB ☐ Master Card ☐ Visa

Account Number _____

Expiration Date _____

Signature _____

May we open a confidential credit card account for you for possible future purchases? ( ) Yes ( ) No

THE HAWORTH PRESS, INC., 10 Alice Street, Binghamton, NY 13904-1580 USA

Please complete the information below or tape your business card in this area.

NAME _____

INSTITUTION _____

ADDRESS _____

CITY _____

STATE _____ ZIP _____

COUNTRY _____

COUNTY (NY residents only) _____

E-MAIL _____

May we use your e-mail address for confirmations and other types of information? ( ) Yes ( ) No. We appreciate receiving your e-mail address and fax number. Haworth would like to e-mail or fax special discount offers to you, as a preferred customer. We will never share, rent, or exchange your e-mail address or fax number. We regard such actions as an invasion of your privacy.

☐ **YES**, please send me **The Therapist's Notebook (ISBN: 0-7890-0400-3)** to consider on a 60-day **no risk** examination basis. I understand that I will receive an invoice payable within 60 days, or that **if I decide to adopt the book, my invoice will be cancelled.** I understand that I will be billed at the lowest price. (Offer available only to teaching faculty in US, Canada, and Mexico.)

Signature _____

Course Title(s) _____

Current Text(s) _____

Enrollment _____

Semester _____ Decision Date _____

Office Tel _____ Hours _____

(14) 08/00   BIC00